JOSEPH E. MURPHY, JR.
Foreword by H. Gifford Fong

THE
RANDOM
CHARACTER
OF INTEREST
RATES

Applying Statistical
Probability to the

Bond Markets

PROBUS PUBLISHING COMPANY
Chicago, Illinois

This publication is designed to provide accurate and authoritative information in regard to the subject matter covered. It is sold with the understanding that the publisher is not engaged in rendering legal, accounting or other professional service. If legal advice or other expert assistance is required, the services of a competent professional person should be sought.

Library of Congress Cataloging in Publication Data Available

ISBN 1-55738-101-1

Printed in the United States of America

1 2 3 4 5 6 7 8 9 0

8-91

To: M. F. M. Osborne

Contents

Preface

This book was designed to serve four purposes: (1) provide a work on the random character of interest rates that could be read from cover to cover; (2) present a viewpoint on interest rates that would serve as a useful framework for understanding the subject; (3) furnish a reference on different kinds of evidence on the random character of interest rates; and (4) establish a foundation for my earlier volume *With Interest* (Dow Jones-Irwin, 1987) which derives the investment implications of the evidence given here.

Because of the large number of technical subjects that had to be covered in presenting the evidence on randomness, the book may not so easily be read from cover to cover. The first several sections can be read fairly easily. Of course, there may be some readers who would gladly devour the entire book in a single reading.

As to the second purpose, providing a framework of interest rates as a random process, I think that viewpoint should be quite clear. Most of the evidence for it is given in graph form, much of it in the first part of the book, and the evidence is quite strong. The evidence does not support a process in which changes in the logarithms of interest rates form a normal distribution of identical and independent random variables. The distribution is only approximately normal and the variance is only approximately stationary. But the evidence does reveal an underlying variable that is approximately random. A strong case can be made, therefore, for making the random walk and approximate Brownian motion the most useful model for viewing interest rates.

The reference material on the evidence of randomness is fairly broad. Some of it is simply the graphic evidence of differencing and log differencing, histograms, nonparametric runs, signs, and other tests. Other evidence concerns the mean, the significance of the mean, the usefulness, if any, of past means as indicators of the future, the reliability of the standard error of estimate for the mean, and the proportion of increases and decreases for various levels of rates. The chapters on these topics treat some fundamental characteristics of the interest rate series. Most of these topics are not treated elsewhere, even though the treatment here is standard statistical practice.

The chapters on the square root of time rule extend the work of M. F. M. Osborne and the author to weekly and daily data, to individual bonds, and to prices. The standard deviation of a random series rises with the square root of time and the presence of this fact in the data is solid evidence that a form of Brownian motion is present. Here the evidence is also extended to the slope of the yield curve, measured as the ratio of short-bond to long-bond yields. This measure obeys the rule, and therefore is a neglected but important fact in understanding the yield curve.

This book does not consider duration, a currently popular topic in the investment community, but I do not feel consideration of duration would alter many of the conclusions reached here. Much of the evidence of this book is based on bond yield indexes which are computed as yields to maturity; part of the evidence dealing with individual bond yields is classified by coupon so that the effects of different durations is minimized.

Acknowledgments

I was privileged to work with Maury Osborne for nearly a decade studying interest rates. This book was inspired by that work and includes some of the material we worked on together. Without Maury, that work would not have been done and this book would not have been written. He has not reviewed this book, and I am solely responsible for any errors.

I am also indebted to Morlin Bree and Susan Freese who provided editorial assistance.

Foreword

Many academic studies focus on the use of data to test theoretical constructs. This approach can provide an important validation of these theoretical constructs. However, a basic examination of data can reveal important theoretical findings. Analysis of the characteristics of the data itself can uncover important principles and relationships.

The Random Character of Interest Rates is a carefully documented and rigorously analyzed study of data describing interest rates. This work is a basic examination of the characteristics of interest rates through the analysis of interest rate data. This remarkable book is Joseph E. Murphy's latest contribution to furthering the understanding of interest rates by robust data analysis.

Some experts believe that spurious conclusions may be drawn in analyzing data without starting from a sound theoretical view. This book does not suffer from such a problem. The comprehensiveness of the data and the thorough statistical and numerical techniques applied preclude any such risk. Moreover, the author's expertise and practical experience ensure a sound application of the methodologies used in the book.

H. Gifford Fong

List of Tables and Figures

Tables

Figures

A NOTE ON THE FIGURES: Most figures in the book consist of multiple graphs. Each graph within a figure is assigned a letter for reference in the text (i.e., graph A, graph B, and so on). The sequence is as follows:

TOP LEFT: **Graph A**	TOP RIGHT: **Graph B**
MID LEFT: **Graph C**	MID RIGHT: **Graph D**
LOWER LEFT: **Graph E**	LOWER RIGHT: **Graph F**

Introduction

There are a great many theories about interest rates; how they operate, what influences them, how they may be predicted, what their relationship is to other economic series, and what underlying characteristics describe the series. Some of these theories are very old; others are comparatively new. Many theories have been developed according to the modern theory of finance, efficiency of the markets, rational expectations, and the like. Some theories are based on an examination of a limited amount of data, the Durand data, for example. Still others are based on no data at all but are drawn primarily from the theoretical framework of how we think things should be, or how they should logically or rationally operate.

Even a quick perusal of the leading journals will show that much of the literature on interest rates is theoretical; little is empirical. Perhaps this lack of empirical basis can be attributed, in part, to the view that science always proceeds from theory to fact, from the theoretical construction of rules that are then tested against data. But, in fact, much of science—perhaps most of it—starts in quite the opposite way, from the data. I would argue that much of modern theory obscures the true nature of the data, certainly more than it clarifies.

No harm would come, it seems, of ignoring the data and looking only to theory, if the use was entirely theoretical. Unfortunately, theories are frequently put to use. I was reminded

1

of this recently when, during a meeting of a college investment committee, a consultant asserted that the future return
on long-term U.S. Government bonds would be 7%—the inflation rate plus 4%—when the actual rate on 30 year U.S.
government bonds was 9%, a disparity of a full 200 basis
points. In this case, theory was substituted for fact in making
an important investment decision.

Across the river, at one of the region's two major banks,
the vice chairman lost $650 million of the bank's assets in
1988, betting on the direction of interest rates following a
similarly disastrous gamble the previous year. Not only the
board of directors of the bank but the Federal Deposit In-
surance Agency and the Comptroller of the Currency were apparently willing to continue to let the vice chairman handle
the depositors' (and, possibly, the taxpayers') money in such
reckless fashion. A careful look at how interest rates behave
would show the folly of such action.

If we had done as much analysis of interest rates and
price data as we have postulated theory, we might not be in
the sorry state of affairs that we are regarding knowledge and
practice in the world of interest rates and bond investment.
The broad literature on interest rates includes few non-
theoretical looks at the data. Most studies begin at too high a
level, aiming to demonstrate that some aspect of a theory is
true or false, rather than to take a close look at how the data
actually behave. An examination of the interest rate series,
conducted without preconception, is essential before we can
climb higher up the tree of knowledge.

Among the current views of interest rates are the following:

- Interest rates are predictable.
- Rates are periodic.
- The long-run rate is a direct function of inflation.
- The yield curve is normally positive.
- Returns on bonds are always less than returns on stocks.
- Changes in interest rates reflect changing expectations.

I would argue that all of these theories except the last are false, and the last is unprovable. I would also argue that, in order to understand interest rates, you must begin with a framework entirely different than that provided by modern capital theory or modern portfolio theory.

In order to understand interest rate and bond-price fluctuation, you must look carefully at the data. If you do that, you will find that the data looks like data provided by stochastic processes, Markov processes, wherein changes in the logs of interest rates resemble a random series. Once you understand the underlying nature of the interest rate series, you can then apply the framework of the bond instrument itself—its fixed coupon, its fixed maturity, and its nearly certain redemption at full value at maturity—to ascertain the risk characteristics of bond investment and bond returns. The latter are only imperfectly and inaccurately portrayed, for example, by the two statistics, mean and variance, and cannot be fit into the common risk return matrix.

To see and comprehend the conflicts between current theory and the reality of the data, we must look carefully at the data. This book is an examination of the underlying data: the interest rates of the past, including how rates have behaved; changes in rates and changes in the logs of rates over varying time intervals for different kinds of bonds and different series, both indexes and individual bonds; and the dispersion and distribution of these changes in rates.

This book is a series of slides or photographs, if you will, snapshots of the character of the data from different perspectives. It is a look at the ratio of increases to decreases, of how or whether that ratio changes for different yield levels, of the standard deviation, of whether the standard deviation is a good measure of future volatility, of whether it changes from one historical period to another and by how much. It is a look at runs or continuous sequences of increases and decreases in the series to see whether such sequences could be attributed to chance or are merely random fluctuations, like coin tossing. It is a look at the comovement of rates, an examination of autocorrelation, an attempt to discover whether lead-lag relationships exist or not.

The aim behind presenting these varied pictures of interest rates is to answer fundamental questions like the following:

Is the series random? Does it exhibit a trend? Are the number of runs, up or down, significantly different than zero? Are rates more likely to drop when they are high, by historical standards, than when they are low? And vice versa? Is their any structure to the yield curve that cannot be explained by random processes? What is the dispersion of changes in rates such as, for example, Brownian Motion? Does the square-root rule hold for the dispersion of interest rates like it does for other random series?

In this book, the data are presented primarily in the form of charts. After looking at these charts for a time, you should get a good idea of the chaotic nature of interest rates, of how difficult it is to predict the particular change in a particular period, but how easy it is to predict the probable change, or the distribution of changes over the long run. Thus, this book approaches the nature of interest rates in the manner introduced nearly a century ago by Louis Bachelier, a French mathematician, whose work was completed and then forgotten for a half century. We take a close look at the underlying data of interest rates and see how they behave.

PART I

Interest Rates and Their Transformations

If yields are a random series in their logarithms, then the first act of analysis, after examining the yield series itself, is to make three transformations. The first transformation is to form first differences in the original yields by subtracting each yield from its successor. The second is to substitute for each yield its logarithm. The third is to form first differences in the logarithms. Transformation to logarithms alters the scale of the original yield series. Taking first differences reveals the randomness in yields. Although these transformations are but alternate ways of looking at the same thing, they form the foundation of later analysis. The final chapter of this section shows why the transformation to logarithms is important.

CHAPTER 1

Overview

The data that form the basis for this book consist of widely used or studied yield indexes; the Salomon U.S. government monthly yield indexes, 1950 to 1986; the Durand annual indexes, 1900 to 1961, the Standard & Poor (S&P) yield indexes, 1900 to 1979; the Macaulay monthly long corporate and commercial yield indexes, 1856 to 1936/1937, and the British consol annual index, 1730 to 1961. We will also examine daily yields and prices of all U.S. bills, bonds, and notes for 1987.

We will consider these interest rate time series from a number of different points of view. We begin with the simple graph of yields. Then we graph first differences in yields, the logs of yields, and first differences in the logs of yields to discover how these different series look in relation to each other. We compare these series in graph form to linear series, periodic series, and random series to observe the similarities and differences.

Linear, periodic, and random series all have quite different characteristics, which may be seen upon visual examination of the graphs. The graphs of an interest rate series, for example, exhibit what seem to be trends and cycles. But when first differences in the series are graphed, the random nature of the series becomes apparent, as does the similarity of the irregularity of yields to the irregularity of randomly generated numbers. The contrast of these series with pure linear series and pure periodic series may also be discerned upon comparing graphs.

Once we have determined that the series is randomlike, we need to evaluate the distribution of the series and the changes in the series. In the second part of the book, we look at the distribution of yields, changes in yields, logs of yields, and changes in logs of yields. The log transformation changes the original series such that the scale of yield does not influence either the original graph of yields or the graph of first differences in yields. Unless we make this transformation, we may observe very large changes in yields when yields are high and very low changes when yields are low, relatively speaking. A separate chapter is devoted to looking at the effect of yield level on the volatility of yields, measured by the standard deviation; in this section, we demonstrate the effects of these highs and lows that we should use logarithms as our basic measure of yields. The distributions of the four alternative measures of yield—original, first difference, log, and log difference—confirm the importance of using logarithms.

A major characteristic of series formed by the cumulation of random numbers is that dispersion, measured by the standard deviation of changes, rises with the square root of time. We investigate the behavior of this characteristic for all series. Such behavior is an indication of randomness. The degree and relation of the standard deviation for different time intervals and different maturity bonds is of both theoretical and practical interest, since it can be used to estimate to a degree of approximation the future volatility of bond yields and bond prices (prices being a function of yield) for different maturity bonds.

An important part of our examination is the volatility of yields versus prices. We will show that, for a perpetuity, the volatility measured by the standard deviation of yields and prices are identical, though of opposite sign, when measured in logs. Very long issues approximate perpetuities in behavior, but short issues have more volatile yields than prices, by definition. The important question is, what is the actual behavior? In this book, we will consider that question using 1987 data.

Not only does the volatility of yields vary by maturity, but it varies by historical period. We examine how the use of logarithms removes much of the difference. We also examine first differences in the logs of yields to determine how much volatility does vary from one era to another, and how nonstationary it is.

Finally, we examine the comovement of interest rates and the characteristics of the yield curve.

By examining interest rates and bond prices in the way we do, we attempt to answer the following questions:

1. What are the underlying characteristics of interest rates?
2. Do interest rate series have a linear trend?
3. Are there regular cycles in interest rates or any indication of periodicity?
4. Are interest rates most appropriately described as "the cumulative sum of random process," a Markov chain?
5. How should we measure interest rates and changes in interest rates: by the original rate or by logarithms?
6. Is the volatility of changes in rates related to the level of yields?
7. What is the dispersion of changes in the logs of interest rates measured by the standard deviation? How does it increase with time?
8. What is the dispersion of bond prices? How does it increase with time? Is it related to the dispersion of yields?
9. Is the volatility of changes in the logs of yields invariant over time? Is the series stationary?
10. How is the volatility of short-term rates related to the volatility of long-term rates?

11. If the changes in interest rates are random, is it possible to predict better than the flip of a coin whether the next change will be up or down?

12. What is the relationship between changes in long and short rates? Is there any lead or lag relationship such that you may be able to predict long-rate changes from short-rate changes, or vice versa?

13. Is there an upper or lower limit to interest rates? Do rates tend to return to a mean? That is, is the series mean reverting?

14. In what ways are all interest rate series alike?

15. In what ways are changes in interest rates similar to changes in bond prices?

16. Does altering the unit of measurement, say from days to months or years, alter the statistical characteristics of the series?

CHAPTER 2

The Record of Interest Rates

Our first look at interest rate data will be the yields themselves as they are printed in the newspaper, or graphed on charts, or even printed in the offering list of a bank or brokerage house. What is given in these reports is the actual yield to maturity at which bonds were offered or sold. These yields form the starting point of our analysis, and we present them first before further breaking them down or transforming them into other series for analysis. Since it is the set of yields we wish to understand through later detailed analysis, we begin with the yields themselves.

Interest rates are typically listed as a set of numbers on a given date for a variety of maturities, most often arranged in chronological order by maturity. The short maturities are at the top of the list, and the long maturities are at the bottom. If you scan the list, you will see that the yields shift rather systematically. For some time, the shorter maturities have had lower yields and the longer maturities higher yields, with a generally smooth rise in yields from short to long. You can see this most clearly when bonds are all of the same type, such as U.S. government bonds.

If we chart yields by maturity, we get a smooth curve (see Figure 2.1); typically, the short maturities are shown on the left of the x axis and the long maturities on the right. In this figure, called the slope of the yield curve, the slope is normally smooth and, more often than not, sloping up to the right.

11

We will investigate why the slope is smooth, how it changes, and whether there is any pattern to the way it changes, or whether the changes in slope are like the random fluctuations of a coin.

Figure 2.1   Yield Curve U.S. Treasury Bonds & Notes, 1987

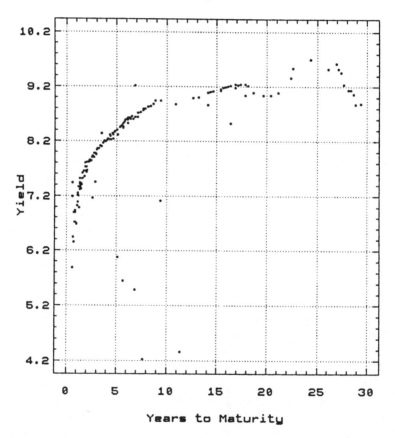

Just as we can plot the yields of many maturities on a single day, so we can plot the yields of a single maturity over many days. Such a plot is a *time series* for that particular maturity. With the exception of perpetuities, or commercial paper rates, it is not possible to plot yields of an actual bond over long time periods because the maturity of the bond continuously declines with time. The alternative is to construct a series of yields for a hypothetically constant maturity bond by averaging the yields of actual bonds of a particular maturity. The most comprehensive indexes of this kind are the Salomon Brothers' constant maturity bond indexes, which go back to 1950 for most series and are available on a monthly basis. Table 2.1 shows a portion of the Salomon yield index for a 3-month U.S. government bill.

Table 2.1   Yields of 3-Month U.S. Securities, 1986

	Jan.	Feb.	Mar.	Apr.	May	Jun.
Yield	7.24	7.18	7.22	6.51	6.25	6.49

If you plot the data in Table 2.2 on a graph, showing the yield each month from 1950 to 1986, you will have the record of the time series. Figure 2.2 records the monthly time series of Salomon yields for six different maturities from 1950 to mid-1986: 3 months and, 1, 2, 5, 10, and 20 years. The figures record the month on the x axis and the level of yields on the y axis.

The graphs in Figure 2.2 reveal several significant characteristics. Perhaps the most significant is the long term upward rise in yields from 1950 to a peak around 1980 and then a decline. At first glance, the rising trend appears to be highly significant. But upon scrutiny it is not as significant as it might seem.

The second feature to consider is the high degree of fluctuation. The series moves up and down in what seems to be a

Figure 2.2   Monthly U.S. Government Yields, 1950–1986

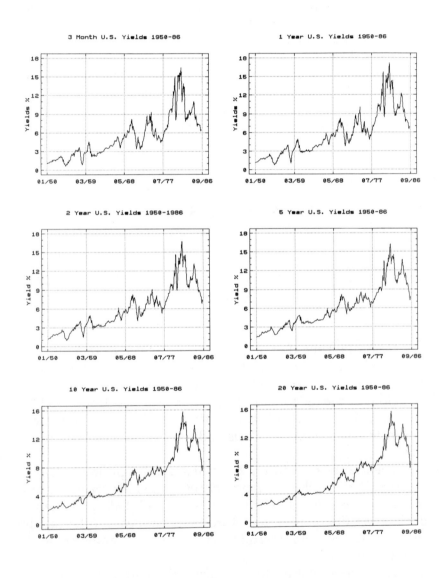

chaotic fashion, suggesting randomness. Yet it is hard to tell from the figure how chaotic, how random those fluctuations are. We will investigate this issue in much more detail to determine whether the fluctuations are random.

The third characteristic of the graphs in Figure 2.2 is clearer and quite remarkable. All of the graphs have the same general pattern: a long-term rise in yields with considerable fluctuation. If you look carefully, you can see that the fluctuations mirror each other to a large degree. The same general pattern characterizes all six series.

The next feature of Figure 2.2 is less easy to discern, but you can see it if you look carefully. If you compare graphs A and F, you can see that the 20-year maturity fluctuates less than the 3-month series. In fact, the longer the maturity, the less the fluctuation. This pattern is difficult to recognize on a time-series chart because the longer maturities have a larger scale than the shorter maturities; thus, a somewhat smaller change on a longer maturity graph occupies the same vertical distance as a larger change on a shorter-maturity graph. Look at the numbers on the y axes (Yield 7) of the graphs. The 10- and 20-year bonds have a high figure of 16%, whereas all the other maturities have a high figure of 18%. We will take a better look at this pattern later when we break down the series.

The final characteristic illustrated in Figure 2.2 is that the degree of fluctuation is much greater toward the end of the period, in the 1970s and early 1980s. If you look carefully, you can see that this higher degree of fluctuation corresponds with a higher level of interest rates; note that, when the fluctuation is greatest, it occurs on the upper part of the chart, not the lower part. Is there a reason for this phenomenon? We will examine the patterns of change to find out.

We can summarize what we have observed from the graphs in Figure 2.2, the six U.S. bond yield series, as follows:

1.   There appears to be an upward trend, but we don't know whether it is significant.

2. There is a great deal of fluctuation, which may be random.
3. All six series seem to follow the same pattern.
4. The longer the maturity, the less the fluctuation.
5. The degree of fluctuation seems to be much greater toward the end, when yields are higher, suggesting a relationship between the level of yield and the degree of fluctuation.

We can use another set of data to check our preliminary observations about the nature of interest rates, the Durand data, annual yields on U.S. corporate bonds from 1900 to 1965. Six of the seven series prepared by Durand are shown in Figure 2.3, they cover 1-, 5-, 10-, 15-, 20- and 25-year maturities. To what extent do they confirm the five observations we made about the Salomon government data?

Our first observation, the existence of an upward trend, is not confirmed because there is no trend in the Durand data. Instead, we see a rise, a fall, a subsequent rise, and a final, very brief fall. We might argue that the series is cyclical, but it would be difficult to say what kind of cycle. So our first observation does not characterize the Durand data.

What about the other four observations? Three of the four seem to be confirmed; evidence for the fourth is unclear in these figures. Namely, there is great deal of fluctuation in the series (2); all six series appear to follow the same general pattern, though to different degrees (3); and the longer the maturity, the less the fluctuation (4). This last pattern is more apparent in the Durand series, since each graph is drawn to the same scale. You can see that the 25-year maturity fluctuates less than the 1-year maturity. But whether the fluctuation is greater at higher levels of yield as suggested by observation 5, is not clear. The Durand data simply do not demonstrate this characteristic; therefore, we will have to defer judgment until we can look at the data from a different perspective. Figures 2.2 and 2.3 present data that cover the twentieth century. What do we know about the characteristics

Figure 2.3   Annual Corporate Yields, 1900–1965

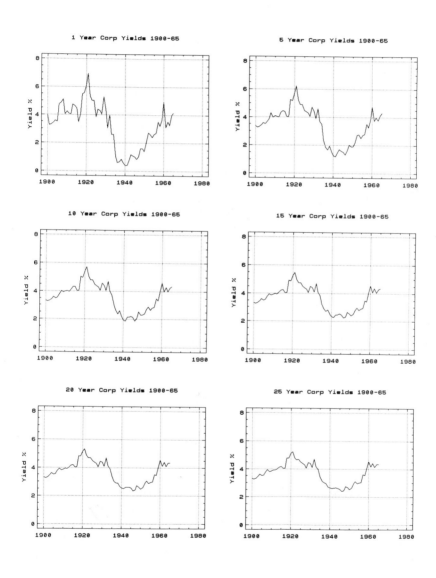

of interest rates in earlier times? Figure 2.4 presents four sets of data from earlier periods. Graphs A and B, from Macaulay, show yields for commercial paper and long-term railroad bonds from 1857 to 1936-1937. If you compare the two, you will see the much more volatile behavior of the commercial paper, the shorter maturity. If you look carefully, you will also see that the volatility seems to be greater during the Civil War period (1861-1865), when yields were much higher, evidence in support of our early observation that volatility may be related to the level of yields. Both series (A and B) reflect more or less continuous volatility.

It is useful to look at the longest series we have, the British consol yields from 1730 to 1961, graph D. There is no overall trend, but there is continuing fluctuation. This series suggests that, whatever the characteristics of interest rates are, they have not changed since the early eighteenth century.

Conclusion

We can definitely conclude that there are at least four characteristics of interest rates:

1. Yields exhibit continuous fluctuation.
2. There appears to be a great deal of comovement among different maturities in the same historical period.
3. In some series, the degree of fluctuation appears to be related to the level of rates.
4. The degree of fluctuation seems to be inversely related to the maturity of the bond.

Although we did see evidence of a trend in some groups of series, we did not in others, which suggests that, while trends may be present, they are definitely not universal.

Figure 2.4 Historical Yields on American and British Bonds

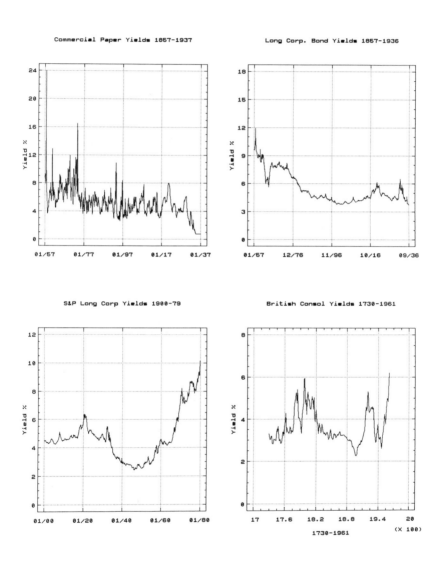

CHAPTER **3**

Changes in Interest Rates

The record of interest rates portrayed in Chapter 2 gave us an overall picture of yields. Based on our observations of the data, we drew several conclusions about the characteristics of interest rates, including the degree of their fluctuation. Granted, our conclusions were general, not detailed, which made it hard to discern the comparative degree of fluctuation among different maturities or between different historical periods and different levels of yield.

We can remedy that deficiency by looking now at changes in yields. We define the change in yield as follows:

$$\Delta y_t = y_t - y_{y-1}$$

Where y_t is the yield at time t and y_{t-1} is the yield at time t − 1. For example, if the yield last month was 11% and the yield this month is 10%, the change in yield is 11 − 10, or 1%. That is an *absolute change* in yield of 1%, where the 1% denotes the actual difference in yields between the two months. We also describe the change in yields as the *first difference* in yields, since we obtain it by subtracting from each yield in the series the preceding yield.

Table 3.1 illustrates first differences in yield.

Table 3.1 Change in Yields of 3-Month U.S. Securities, 1986

	Jan.	Feb.	Mar.	Apr.	May	Jun.
Change in Yield	–.12	–.06	.04	–.71	–.26	.24

You can see how different the changes are from the yields themselves.

The change series represents quite a different kind of series than the original yield series, even though we can reconstruct the original yield series from the change series, given the first yield.

The set of graphs in Figure 3.1 shows changes (first differences, actually) in yields for the six U.S. bond indexes we portrayed earlier. This series illustrates some quite remarkable features, only some of which were evident in the series in Chapter 2. For instance:

1. There is an enormous amount of fluctuation. It is similar for all six maturities in terms of when it occurred and its degree.
2. The scale in the y axis is not the same for all figures. The range of values (visible on the left scale) is far greater for the short maturities than for the long.
3. The fluctuation is much higher in the late 1970s and 1980s than in the 1950s (i.e., much more fluctuation when the level of yields was much higher).
4. There are about as many increases as decreases, and the increases and decreases in any period are of approximately the same magnitude.
5. The magnitude of change appears to be different in some historical periods when the level of yields was similar.

We observed some of features in our analysis in Chapter 2, but now they are demonstrated much more clearly. Note that the last two observations are new: (4) the apparently

Figure 3.1 First Differences in U.S. Government Yields, 1950–1986

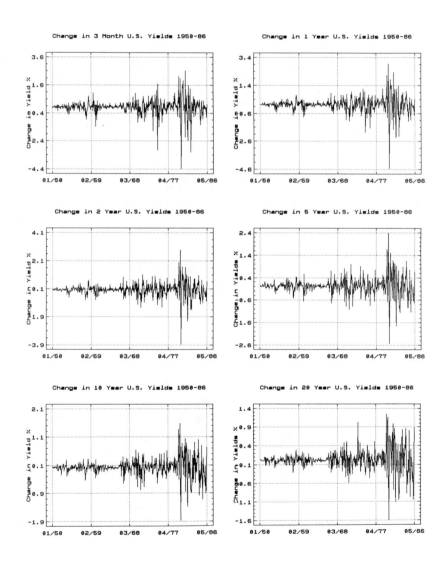

equal occurrence of increases and decreases and (5) historical differences in magnitude. Perhaps the most startling observation made of these graphs is how utterly Similar they seem, not only in the general pattern they follow but in the details of the data as well.

Figure 3.2 includes the four historical series examined earlier: the Macaulay data (graphs A and B), the S&P long corporate yields, and the consol yields. Each figure is drawn to a different scale, which emphasizes the similarities between the patterns. You can see that the commercial paper series (A) and the long corporate bond series (B) are very similar. Actually, all four graphs exhibit most of the characteristics observed of the other figures. Again, there is the random fluctuation that prevailed in the Salomon U.S. government bonds. In brief, we see considerable fluctuation, as many increases as decreases, similarity of magnitude of increases and decreases, and some differences in historical periods. A final observation is that it would be very difficult to predict with better than 50% probability the direction of the next change based on past changes. Nor could we tell the magnitude of change. In this respect, the series of changes might be characterized as a very random series.

First Differences With Constant Scale

Figures 3.1 and 3.2 were drawn to different scales to demonstrate the striking similarities among series drawn from the same historical era. The next set of figures (3.3 and 3.4) are drawn to the same scale for each group to show the effect of maturity on the degree of fluctuation. Obviously, it was not possible to show both characteristics in the same set of figures.

Figure 3.3 presents the Salomon series, the six U.S. bond series of yields from 1950 to 1986, with all figures drawn on the same scale. You can see at once how the degree of fluctuation lessens as the maturity increases. There is a progressive drop in volatility as we move from the 3-month maturity to the 20-year maturity. In every period, the long maturities

Figure 3.2 First Differences in Historical Yields

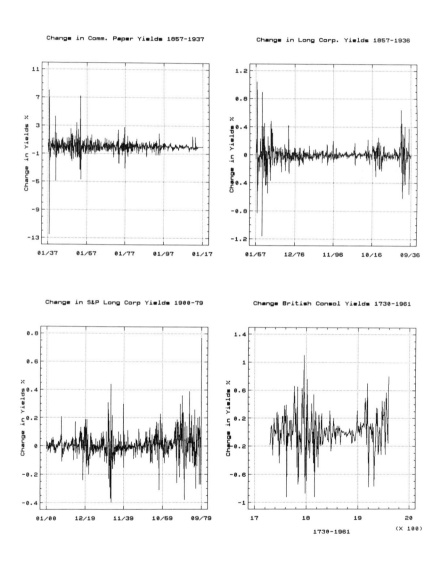

26   Part I

Figure 3.3   First Differences in U.S. Government Yields, 1950–1986, Uniform Scale

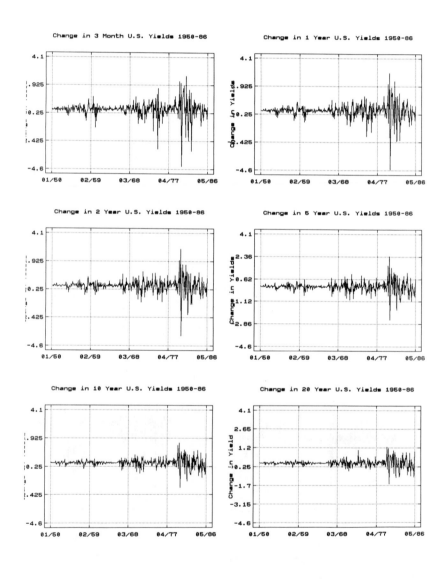

Figure 3.4   First Differences in Historical Yields—
            Uniform Scale

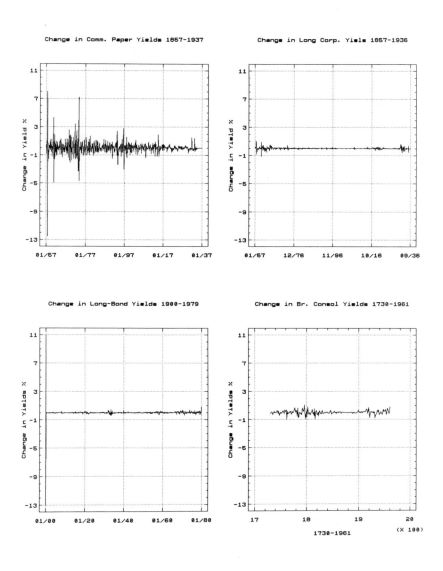

exhibit much more fluctuation than the short. In addition, the volatility is much greater in the latter part of the period, when yields are much higher.

In Figure 3.4 we show the Macaulay data, together with the British consol data and long-term U.S. bonds from 1900 to 1979 all drawn to the same scale. The scale on the consol data has been adjusted to reflect that it is annual data, rather than monthly data. The adjustment puts all four graphs on the same basis. You can see in Figure 3.4 how the same inverse relationship between degree of fluctuation and maturity appears in these series. The long U.S. bond yields and the British consol yields are much less volatile than the commercial paper yields.

Conclusion

We can summarize our observations of the data in this chapter as follows:

1. Volatility of change in interest rates characterizes all periods but seems to differ somewhat from one period to the next.
2. Volatility is higher when yields are higher.
3. Yields of long bonds are less volatile than yields of short bonds.
4. The pattern of volatility in the same historical period is very similar for all maturities.
5. There appear to be as many increases as decreases in yield.
6. The magnitude of increases and decreases is similar in any given period.

We have discovered the general pattern, but the details remain. We need to know how much volatility changes from one period to the next, what the effect of the level of yields is and how it might be removed, the exact degree to which increases and decreases are equal, and whether they are affected by the level of yields. But first, we must determine whether we can remove the effect of level of yield. That is the issue we will turn to next.

CHAPTER 4

Logs of Interest Rates

In the last chapter, we found that by taking first differences in a series yields, we obtained a new series which exhibited more uniform characteristics than the original series even though the two series, the original series and the first difference series, were inverses of one another. That is to say, the one could be transformed in to the other by the difference operator, or its inverse. Not only did taking first differences give us a more homogeneous series, it permitted us to see features of the series that were not so evident before.

Another transformation which is equally useful is the logarithmic transformation, or the log transformation for short. In this transformation we substitute for each interest rate of the series the natural logarithm of that interest rate. The log transformation will bring out another side of yields and give us new insights. The importance of using logs is suggested by the fact that in computing risk in trading options on U.S. Treasury bills, traders always use the log transformation.

An important advantage of using logarithms is that the difference between two values of a series is always the same when the percentage change is the same. Consequently, if you graph a series on a figure, equal percentage changes in the series will always produce precisely the same vertical distance. Even more convenient when we use natural logs is the fact that, for changes between –15% and +15%, the percentage change and the log change are approximately the same. A log change of –.10 is –10%, and a log change of +.10 is +10%.

Recall from Chapters 2 and 3 that the volatility of interest rates appeared to rise when the level of rates rose. This suggests that the volatility of rates is proportional to the level of rates. If this is the case, as it is with many or perhaps most economic series, then converting interest rates into their logarithms will homogenize the data, so to speak. Changes in the logs of rates will not be affected by scale as changes in the actual rates appear to be.

The first six graphs in Figure 4.1 present the Salomon yields, 1950 to 1986. You can see that the degree of volatility is much more uniform over the series than it was in the figures of the actual yields (Chapter 3). But other more subtle differences are observed if you compare Figure 4.1 with the figures in Chapter 3. In the figure for the 3-month maturity, for example, note that there is more volatility depicted in the 1950s than in the 1980s. This is the reverse of the situation depicted in the actual yield figures, where the 1980s volatility was much greater than the 1950s volatility.

What does this mean? When we homogenize the data by using logs, we get a very different picture. What we've observed about the 3-month bill yields is also true of all the other U.S. yields in Figure 4.1, except perhaps the 20-year bond. Even so, the 20-year bond, as portrayed on a log scale is much different than the same bond portrayed on an arithmetic scale.

Somewhat the same transformation occurs when we examine the Durand data, in Figure 4.2. We now see the much greater volatility in the Durand yields of the long bonds than we did on the arithmetic scale. Compare the long bonds on the two sets of figures, Figure 4.2 and Figure 3.3. It is important to remember that the scales of the log figures differ. The scale on the 1-year Durand figure covers a much wider range than the scale on the 25-year bond, which hides the fact that the short bond has a much more volatile yield.

The point to be made for the log figures is that the pattern of volatility is approximately the same for all six maturities over the entire span, a fact that is not demonstrated by the arithmetic scale. There is a commonality here that

Figure 4.1 Logarithms of U.S. Government Yields, 1950–1986

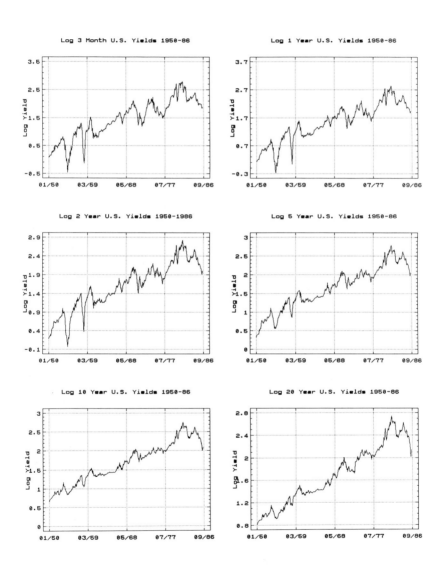

Figure 4.2   Logarithms of Corporate Yields, 1900–1965

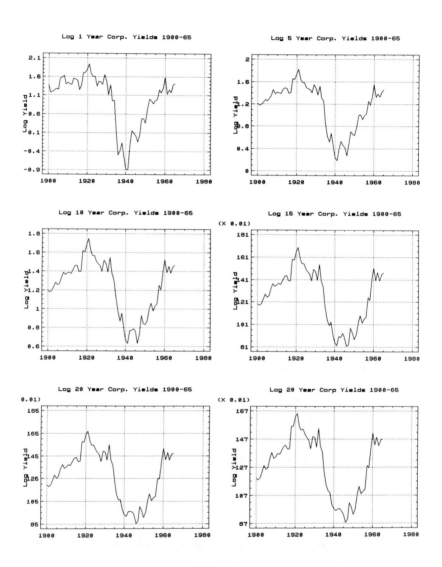

graphs of the original yields do not reveal. Figure 4.3 covers the two Macaulay sets of data and the British consol and S&P long data. Use of logs for this data is particularly appropriate because of the great range in scale, especially for the Macaulay data. For the long-bond Macaulay data (1857-1936), there is far more volatility than appeared in the arithmetic figure (Figure 2.4). In fact, the volatility of the long bond is maintained throughout the entire period.

Conclusion

Any series of yields for a particular bond may be transformed into the logs of yields and the logs of yields can, by the inverse transformation, be converted back to the original yields.

1. The log transformation is extremely important because it converts a yield series whose degree of fluctuation (or variance) is much higher when yields are high than when they are low into a series whose volatility is not dependent on the level of yields.

2. When we remove the arbitrary effect of level of yield from the interest rates series, we obtain a graph of yields which reveals a pattern quite different from that of the graph of the original yields.

3. The degree of fluctuation in the logs of yields appears to be more equal over time.

4. The sharp changes in volatility that had appeared in the original yield series are now seen to be largely a function of scale, or of the level of yields.

Figure 4.3   Logarithms of Historical Yields

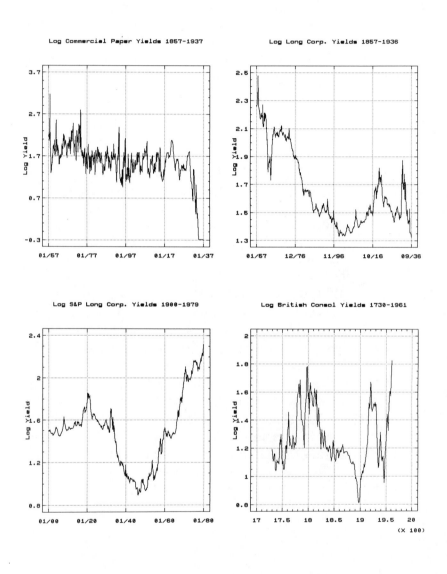

CHAPTER 5

Changes in the Logs
of Interest Rates

The graphs of the logs of interest rates given in Chapter 4 gave a very different picture than the graphs of the original rates given in Chapter 2; just the changes in rates of Chapter 3 gave a perspective on rates very different from the perspective of the original series. Each transformation, differencing and conversion to logs, uncovered a new aspect of interest rates. In this chapter, we wish to combine the transformations of the last two chapters, conversion to logs and taking first differences in the logs of yields. In making the double transformation we can remove the effect of the level of rates and then see clearly the degree of function of rates, unaffected by level, for different periods and different maturities. The doubly transformed variable will show us whether the degree of fluctuation remained constant over long periods and how the fluctuation varied by maturity. We will be able to see in general terms whether the variance was constant over time and how the variance shifted as the maturity of the yield series did. If the variance for the same maturity is constant over time, the series is called homoscedastic; if the variance is not constant, the series is called heteroscedastic.

We should be able to answer most of these questions by looking carefully at the figures. Figure 5.1 presents the six maturities of Salomon yields, 1950 to 1986. Perhaps the most striking feature of the graphs in this figure is observed when we compare them with those in Figure 4.1, the changes-in-yield figure. In Figure 5.1, the log-change figure, there is no longer a high degree of fluctuation concentrated in the latter part of the period, on the right of each graph. Instead, there is high fluctuation throughout, with no skewing in heavy fluctuation at one end of the figure or the other. In Figure 4.1, the change-in-yield figure, you will see the sharp contrast with the change in logs of yield series.

What has happened is that we have removed the effects of scale by taking log differences in yields, rather than actual differences. The difference is quite pronounced. We should note that the sharp difference in these figures arose only because the level of yields was not the same throughout the 1950 to 1986 period but shifted greatly. With a more homogeneous set of yields, we would not have seen this contrast.

Now let's turn to the second question we raised above. Is the degree of fluctuation about the same throughout? Clearly, it is not. Scan each graph in Figure 5.1, and note that each is divided into four panels. You will see that the degree of fluctuation in the second panel is less than in the first, third, and fourth panels. There is a definite decline in volatility in the mid-1960s. This suggests very strongly that the series is not time invariant. The historical period makes a difference.

We can see an interesting feature of the shifts in degree of fluctuation. The same shifts, the same pattern, characterizes all six maturities. All have lower degrees of fluctuation in the second part of the time span and more in the first, third, and fourth. Even a casual glance over the graphs will show that correspondence. Clearly, as revealed by first differences in logs, the pattern of degree of fluctuation is similar for all maturities. Note that, on these figures, the scale is not the same for each maturity.

A much broader range of values is encompassed in the 3-month maturity than in the 20-year maturity. But if we overlook that fact, as we do in this figure, the pattern seems to be the same.

Figure 5.1 First Difference in Logarithms of U.S. Government Yields, 1950–1986

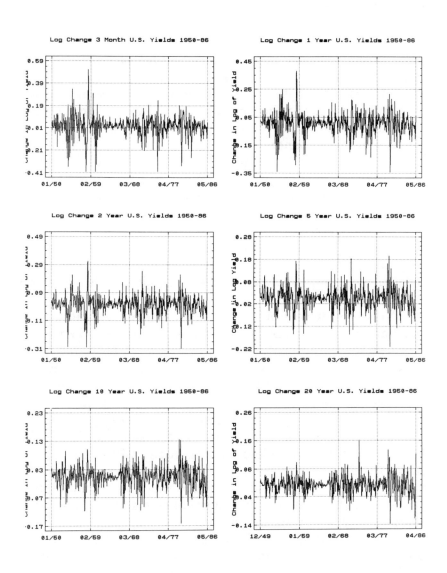

A rough comparison of the number of lines above and below zero change suggests that positive and negative changes are roughly equal in number. The chance of a rise in rates is about the same as a fall, one-half in each case. This is what we might expect.

That brings us to the third question: What is the distribution of changes in the logs of rates? You can see that there are a few extreme changes and also many small changes. In addition, the pattern above the zero line looks comparable to the pattern below, suggesting that the distribution is symmetrical. We will have to look at that more carefully when we look at the histogram of changes in yields.

Next, let's look at Figure 5.2, the Macaulay, S&P, and British consol data. Again, we have a picture of randomlike behavior: roughly as many increases as decreases, little means to tell whether the next change will be up or down, and differences between periods. There is less conformity here between the Macaulay commercial paper and the Macaulay long-bond series. There is clear evidence of the higher volatility of the commercial paper, even though each is drawn on a different scale.

Now, to answer our last question: Are the patterns of fluctuation the same or similar for all maturities? When we plot differences in logarithms on figures with the same scale, we can see how volatility is related to maturity. The previous figures were all on different scales, so we could not tell what the effect of maturity was unless we looked very carefully at the legend on the y axis. In Figure 5.3, the set of graphs uses the same scale for each maturity. The first group is for the U.S. Salomon indexes. Note that the degree of volatility, indicated by the displacement made by the lines, declines as maturity rises. The 20-year bonds are much less volatile than the 3-month bills. In fact, the degree of change in logs declines continuously with each longer maturity.

The last graphs plotted on the same scale are those in Figure 5.4, the Macaulay commercial paper and long-bond series, 1857 to 1936/1937. You can see the sharp difference in volatility between the short and the long.

Figure 5.2 First Difference in Logarithms of Historical Yields

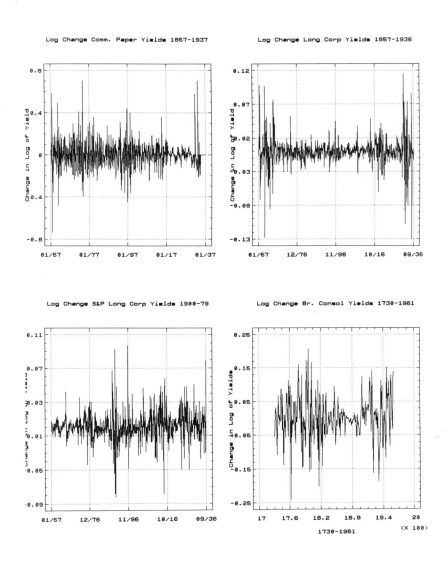

Figure 5.3   First Difference in Logarithms of U.S. Government Yields, 1950–1986—Uniform Scale

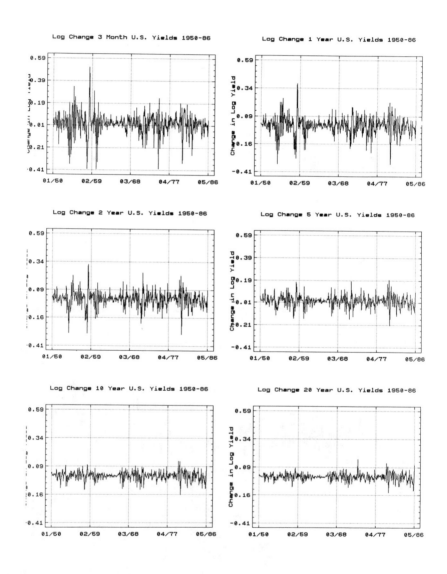

Figure 5.4 First Difference in Logarithms of Historical Yields—Uniform Scale

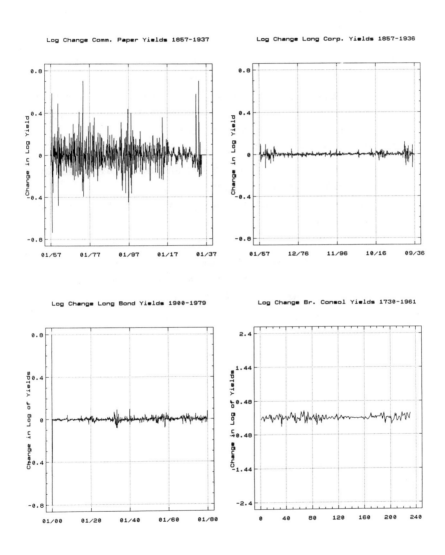

Conclusion

How can we summarize what we have found in looking at changes in the logs of yields? A number of observations can be made, and, in making them, we will use the word volatility to describe the degree of change in the logs of yields.

1. Clearly, scale has an impact on volatility, and measurement in logs removes this.
2. All series are highly volatile and the nature of the volatility (but not the degree) is similar for all maturities and all time periods.
3. Volatility is not the same in all historical periods.
4. The volatility pattern in the same historical period is similar for all maturities.
5. Short maturities are much more volatile than long maturities.
6. Past changes cannot be used to predict whether future changes will be positive or negative.
7. The numbers of positive and negative changes appear to be approximately equal.
8. There are more small than large changes.

CHAPTER **6**

How the Level of Interest Rates Affects Interest Rate Volatility

In the previous chapter we saw that conversion to logs makes interest rate data far more homogeneous. After the log transformation, the degree of change in yields, the volatility, is no longer a direct function of the level of yields, but now seems much more independent of yield level. Our knowledge of this is based on general observation.

In this chapter we wish to test what the figures of the two previous chapters suggest, (1) that prior to the log transformation volatility was related to the level of yields and (2) that we have removed the effect of level of yields on the degree of volatility.

Let us look first at some figures showing monthly changes in interest rates over the last quarter of a century—the period 1950 to 1986. This period was a time of rising rates, a time in which U.S. Government yields rose from 2-3% in the 1950's to more than 16% by 1981—a height not reached previously since the Civil War.

If the volatility of rates is related to the level of rates, we would expect to see higher volatility, a higher degree of monthly changes in rates in the late 1970's and early 1980's than in the 1950's. Graphs A and B of Figure 6.1 suggest that

Figure 6.1   First Differences, First Differences in Logarithms, and Yields of U.S. Government Bonds, 1950–1986

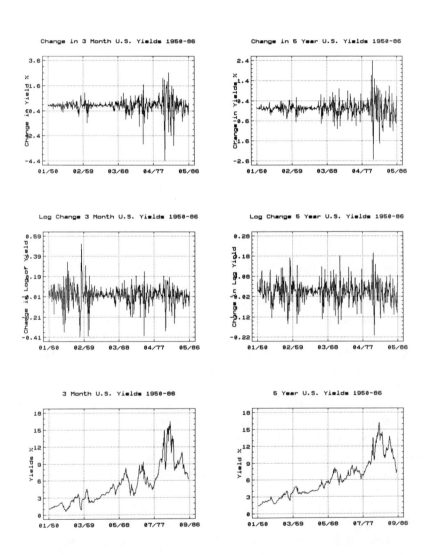

changes in rates were much greater in the late 70's and early 80's than in the 1950's. The monthly changes are much higher in the later period, the right side of the figure, than in the earlier periods, the left side. The higher volatility in the later period is true of both short and long maturities as can be seen in the figures of Chapter 1. The greater changes correspond to the higher interest rates prevailing in the late 1970's and 1980's, depicted in Graphs E and F of Figure 6.1

The degree of volatility will be seen to be proportional to the level of rates, and we can remove the effect of the level of rates by measuring changes in rates in natural logarithms, a transformation that makes all changes proportional to the level. A rise in interest rates from 5% to 6% is the same proportional change, and the same log change, as a rise from 10% to 12%, or a natural log change of 0.18 in each case.

Let's see what happens when we graph monthly changes in logs instead of actual changes. Graphs C and D of Figure 6.1 show this for the 3-month bill and 5-year bonds. You can see that there is no longer any difference in volatility between the 1950's and the late 1970's and early 1980's. You can see that the degree of volatility is about the same. These charts give a basis for believing that changes in rates are proportional to the level of rates.

We can be more general in our measurement by computing the standard deviation, a measure of volatility, for changes in actual yields and for changes in the natural logarithms of yields. If the former is related to the level of rates, and the latter is not, the standard deviation of changes in interest rates will rise with the rise in rates, but the standard deviation of changes in the natural logarithms of rates will remain unaffected.

The graphs of Figure 6.2 show the divergent effects for various maturity securities and for different periods of history. We calculated the standard deviation of all changes in yield when yields were 2% (2.0–2.9%). Since yields may have been 2–2.9% in different periods, the standard deviation may be based on a mix of historical periods. To eliminate small samples, no standard deviation was calculated when we had less than ten changes. We made the same calculation when yields were 3–3.9%, 4–4.9%, and so on. For each yield level, we computed two standard deviations: (1) the standard deviation of changes in nominal yields, and (2) the standard deviation of changes in the natural logarithms of yields.

In the figure you can see that whereas the standard deviation of changes in yields rises with the rise in yield levels, the other measure does not rise. The effect of the level of yields is removed when we measure changes using logs. When we eliminate the impact of proportionality by the log transformation, the volatility is roughly alike for all yield levels.

Note that one of the graphs, that for the British consol, goes back to 1730, two and a half centuries ago, yet the impact of level of rates on volatility remains present, suggesting a permanent characteristic. Some of the graphs are for short term bills; others are for long term bonds. Some cover the latter 19th century and early 20th century; others are for the second half of the 20th century. Yet all, for each time period and for all maturities, reveal that the volatility of changes in interest rates is proportional to the level of rates.

What is the significance of this? First, the level of rates has great impact on the volatility of income for a lender or investor. In high yield periods nominal rates will change more so that the impact on dollar and cents income will be much greater. There will be a corresponding effect on the market values of long bonds. At high yield levels, bond prices are much more volatile because the point change in yield is much greater.

Second, if we want to determine the degree of change volatility of interest rates, we must distinguish what part of the change is simply due to a shift in the level of interest rates and what is due to changes after the level effect has been removed.

If a distribution is lognormal, the standard deviation of first differences in the original series, Δx, will be proportional to the mean; the standard deviation of first differences in the log series, Δy, will not be proportional to the mean. We have just seen that that is true in general. Now we wish to test the question more precisely. In making the test, we hypothesize the standard deviation (s.d.) to be equal to the mean unit standard deviation ($\underline{s}$/yield) times the yield. In other words, s.d. = yield × unit standard deviation. The unit standard deviation is the standard deviation for each yield range divided by the midpoint of that yield range, averaged over all yield ranges. We then computed the coefficient of correlation between actual standard deviations and hypothesized standard deviations and used a t-test to determine whether the relationship is significant. This is a more stringent test than simply regressing the standard deviations on the yield range midpoints.

If changes in yields are a lognormal distribution, then we expect to find a significant relationship for the actual first differences, Δx. On the other hand, we expect to find no relationship between the standard deviation and the level of yields for the log first differences, Δy. The yield series, all monthly, are as follows:

1. Commercial paper, 1857-1937, Macaulay
2. Long-term corporate yields, 1867-1936, Macaulay
3. Long-term high-grade corporate yields, 1938-1979, Standard & Poor
4. 3-month U.S. yields, 1958-1977, Standard & Poor
5. 3-month U.S. government yields, 1950-1986, Salomon
6. 1-year U.S. government yields, 1950-1986, Salomon
7. 2-year U.S. government yields, 1950-1986, Salomon
8. 5-year U.S. government yields, 1950-1986, Salomon
9. 10-year U.S. government yields, 1950-1986, Salomon
10. 20-year U.S. government yields, 1950-1986, Salomon
11. 30-year U.S. government yields, 1953-1986, Salomon

In making each test, we examined the data shown in Figure 6.2

Figure 6.2   The Level of Yield and the Standard Deviation of Changes in the Logarithms of Yields, Selected Yields

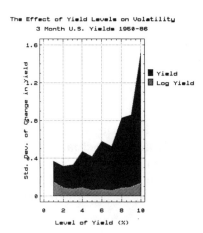

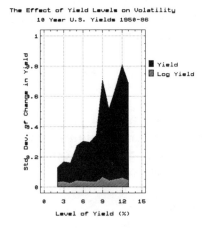

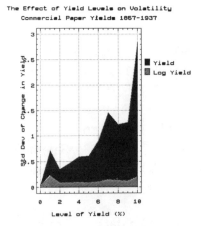

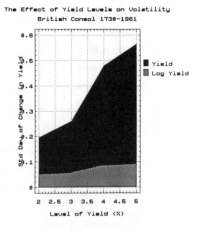

Table 6.1   Tests to Determine Whether the Standard Deviation of First Differences in Yields and of First Differences of Logs of Yields are Proportional to the Mean

	Yields (Δx)			Logs of Yields (Δy)	
Series	R-Square	t-test		R-Square	t-test
1	.73	4.17*		0.15	0.47
2	.65	2.46*		0.00	0.01
3	.72	3.31*		0.17	0.47
4	.92	6.56*		0.49	1.35
5	.75	4.26*		0.02	0.07
6	.96	14.56*		0.35	1.23
7	.81	5.51*		0.02	0.06
8	.93	11.27*		0.46	2.09
9	.89	8.42*		0.49	2.14
10	.90	8.87*		0.61	3.05*
11	.86	7.21*		0.37	1.46

*Significantly different than zero at the 5% level of significance.

The results are shown in Table 6.1. The table clearly shows that the standard deviation of first differences in yields (Δx) are significantly related to the level of yields (at the 5% level), as shown in the second and third columns. All of the t-test values are significant at the 5% level of significance.

The table also shows that the standard deviation of first differences in the logs of yields (Δy) are not significantly related to the level of yields (columns 4 and 5). Only one of the t-test values is significant.

Conclusion

Based on the evidence of the relationship between the level of yields and the standard deviation of changes in yields and the logs of yields, we may conclude:

1. The degree of change in yields, or the volatility of yields, is directly related to the level of yields.
2. The degree of change in the logs of yields is not related to the level of yields.
3. We can homogenize interest rate data by transforming yields into the their logs and thereby obtain a series whose variance is more stationary.
4. In analyzing the underlying characteristics of interest rates, the logs of the series should be used, otherwise the results will be affected by shifts in yield levels.
5. When yields are high, shifts in yield will have a much greater impact on the income of investors and lenders and on the costs to borrowers than when yields are low because the shifts tend to be proportional to the level of yields.
6. The proportional effect of interest rate changes is unaffected by the level of yields.

PART II

The Frequency Distribution of Interest Rates

In the last section we kept interest rates and their transformations in the order in which they occurred over time. In this section, we count the number of changes of similar magnitude and form the frequency distribution of those changes. Though in so doing, we destroy the original order, the new distributions enable us to generalize the pattern of changes and give us the tools for making probability predictions of future changes. The new distributions also permit us compare and contrast the yields, and their transformations, with the distributions of linear, periodic, and random series, described in Appendix A. Interest rate distributions are similar to random distributions, not to linear or periodic distributions.

CHAPTER 7

Frequency Distributions

We have just seen that by making the log transformation, we homogenize the data. We have also that we can remove the effect of yield levels on the variance or volatility of yields by this log transformation. The impact of yields becomes important when we look at the next important aspect of yields and changes in yields, their distribution.

In examining a set of data, one of the first things to do is to look at the profile of the data, the frequency distribution. The frequency distribution can often reveal the underlying nature of the data

The frequency distribution of a set of numbers is determined by dividing the numbers into various classes, or ranges, counting the number of numbers in each range and listing how frequently each number occurs.

A frequency distribution gives us important information. For example, it not only tells us what kind of series of numbers we are dealing with but also may enable us to make certain kinds of predictions about future numbers in the series. Certainly, for interest rates, anything that will enable us to make predictions is of great importance. Even if we cannot predict, any help we can gain in knowing what kind of numbers we have will be extremely useful.

Before turning to interest rates, it is useful to describe the frequency distributions of two major series, the linear series and the periodic series. The linear series is exemplified by the set of integers: 1, 2, 3, 4, and so on. Any linear series may be reduced to a function of the set of integers by applying the equation $y = a + bx$, where y is the liner series we wish to describe and x is the set of integers. The frequency distribution of the linear series is a uniform distribution. The frequency of each integer and of each equal range of integers is the same; that is, all frequencies are the same. Whenever we have a linear series, we will have a distribution that is linear or approximately linear.

The distribution of first differences of a linear series is not uniform but unimodal. There is a single range, and the frequency in that range is the total of the number of items in the series. The first difference of the series 1, 2, 3 is the series 1, 1, 1. The frequency distribution of that set is 3 ones. By simply looking at the frequency distribution of a series or first differences in the series, we can tell whether the series is linear.

A periodic series is a series in which values repeat themselves. A regular-period series is a series in which the repeated segments are equivalent. An example is the series 1, 2, 1, 2, 1, 2, 1. The frequency distribution of this series is again uniform but of limited range. Here, the range is 1 to 2. The first differences in the above series are +1, −1, +1, −1, +1, −1. The frequency distribution of the first differences is 3 + 1 and 3 − 1. The distribution is not unimodal but uniform—in this case, bimodal. A sine series is an example of a periodic series. The frequency distributions of both the original series of sines and the first differences in the series will both be uniform.

While we can recognize both a linear series and a periodic series by their graphs, we can also use frequency distributions to determine their nature. A linear series has a uniform distribution; first differences in the series have a unimodal distribution. A periodic series has a uniform and possibly bimodal distribution; first differences have a uniform and possibly bimodal distribution.

When we turn to a random series, we obtain something entirely different. The most well-known random series is generated by flipping coins assigning +1 to heads and −1 to tails, and calculating the results in a running sum. The result is a graph that looks very much like that of interest rates or the stock market, for that matter. The graph of the series is clearly neither linear nor periodic but may, at times appear to be linear, periodic, or a combination of both. If we take differences in the cumulative series down to the smallest difference, we will have a bimodal distribution consisting of −1 and +1. The expected frequencies of each number +1 and −1 are equal, though the probability of getting precisely the expected number, contrary to intuition, is quite low and declines with the number of flips. If we take differences at intervals greater than 1, we obtain a symmetric distribution that approaches the normal distribution as the intervals and the length of the series increase toward infinity. If we have 100 flips in each difference, the frequency of obtaining 100 tails or 100 heads is very small, giving +100 or −100, respectively. Much more likely is a figure closer to zero. The net result is a distribution of first differences that is bell shaped, symmetrical, and, in the long run, normal. The original series, however, is not necessarily normal but will tend to be.

By looking at the frequency distribution of the series and first differences in the series, we can tell what kind of series we have: linear, periodic, or random. If the distribution of the original series is uniform and the distribution of first differences unimodal, we have a linear series. If the distribution of both the original series and first differences is uniform or roughly so, we have a periodic series. But if the distribution of the series and particularly of first differences in the series is normal or approximately so, we have a random series. Sometimes, the first differences in the logarithms of the series are normal, then we have a log-normal series. The logs of the series are normal and changes in the logs are random.

Figure 7.1 shows the Salomon U.S. yields, 1950 to 1986. The frequency distributions in Figure 7.1 give the number of times each yield occurred for intervals of 0.0 to 0.9%, 1.0 to 1.9%, and so on. For each graph in the figure, there is also a line of the normal distribution. For a series that is log-normal (i.e., the first differences in the logs are approximately normal), the distribution of actual yields will not necessarily be normal. There will tend to be, moreover, a long tail to the

Figure 7.1   Histograms of Yields, Logarithms of Yields, First Differences in Yields, & First Differences in the Logarithms of Yields, U.S. Bonds, 1950–1986

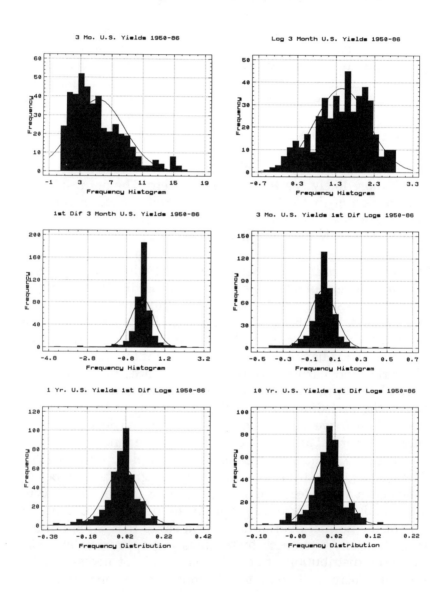

right, reflecting that the underlying changes are log-normal. Quite clearly, the yields themselves are not normal.

Graphs A, B, C, and D of Figure 7.1 give data for 3-month maturities. Graph A gives the frequency distribution of reported yields. The graph is skewed to the left, toward the lower yields, and is not symmetric and not normal. Graph B of Figure 7.1 gives the frequency distribution of the logarithms of yields. The graph is now skewed to the right, again not symmetric, and not normal, though it is more normal than Graph A. Graph C shows the distribution of first difference in yields. This graph is now nearly symmetric and much more normal. Graph D gives the distribution of changes in the logarithms of yields and, like Graph C, is more symmetric, more normal. Graphs E and F show the frequency distributions of first differences in the logs of 1-year and 10-year bonds. They too reveal distributions having much more symmetry and normality than the graphs of yields or logarithms of yields, neither of which is shown.

Figure 7.2 shows data for British consols from 1730 to 1961 and for commercial paper and long bonds 1857 to 1936/7. All of the data are monthly, except the British consol, which are annual. Graphs A, C, and E give the distributions of yields, revealing marked skewness to the left for all three series. Graphs B, D, and F give the distributions for first differences in the logarithms of yields. These graphs are generally symmetric and much more normal than the graphs of the yields.

From the frequency distribution we can form the cumulative frequency distribution. When expressed in percent, the cumulative frequency distribution gives the percentage for each cumulative relative frequency. For a normal distribution, the graph will be a straight line, extending from lower left to upper right. For a distribution that has excessive frequencies in the center, the graph will bulge upward in the center. Finally, a narrow distribution has long tails and has a high center that will result in a shape like an S-curve. In that case, there will be more items close to the mean and more at the extremes

Figure 7.2   Histograms of Yields and First Differences in the Natural Logarithms of Yields, Historical Data

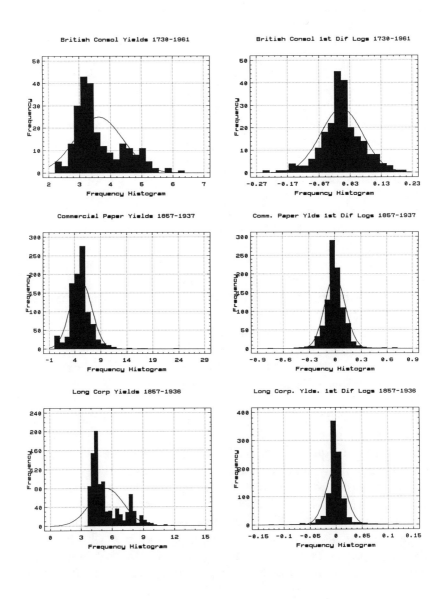

than in a normal distribution. Figures 7.3 and 7.4 present the cumulative relative frequency distributions for selected yield series and random numbers.

Figure 7.3 shows the cumulative frequency distributions for yields. The figure reveals marked departures from the normal curve evidenced by departures from a straight line. The random walk series gives the closest approximation to a straight line, but even this reveals departures, as may be expected in the exponents of the running cumulation of random numbers.

Figure 7.4 gives the cumulative frequency distribution for first differences in the logs of yields. The random series in Graph B is now almost a perfect straight line, as are Graphs A (Consol yields) and F (20-Year U.S. Yields). Graph D and E still reveal the S-curve outline evidencing more than the expected number of extreme changes. Overall, the first differences in logarithms of Figure 7.4 are much more normal than the yields of Figure 7.3.

Conclusion

What do the frequency distributions tell us about interest rates?

1. The distribution of yields has too many yields in the center and an excess in the higher yields, suggesting that the log transformation may give a more symmetrical distribution.
2. The distribution of the logs of yields is more symmetrical, more normal.
3. The distribution of changes in yields is peaked with wide tails.
4. The distribution of first differences in the logs of yields is also peaked, with wide tails, and symmetrical. The mean is very close to zero.

Figure 7.3   Normal Probability Plot of Selected Yields and Random Numbers

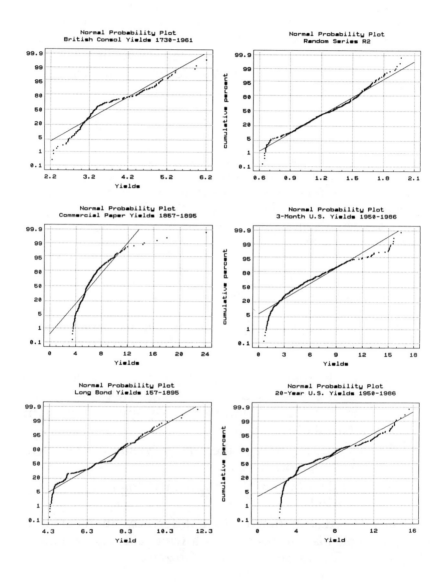

Figure 7.4   Normal Probability Plot of Yields and First Differences in the Natural Logarithms of Yields, Selected Bonds and Random Numbers

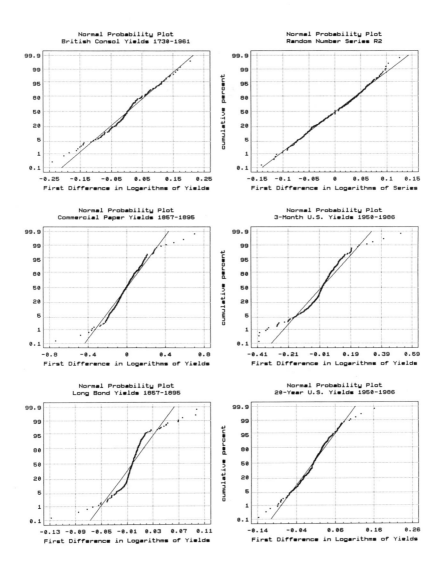

The cumulative frequency distributions reveal the same pattern. This indicates that:

1. The expected change in yields is zero.
2. Small changes in yields are much more likely than moderate changes.
3. Extreme changes in yields, plus or minus, are more common than we would expect from a normal distribution. This pattern, it is interesting to note, also occurs with stock prices.

CHAPTER 8

Is the Distribution of Interest Rates Normal or Lognormal?

A lognormal distribution is a distribution in which the logs of the variate are normal, or approximately normal, as distinguished from a distribution in which the variate itself is normal. Thus, if $y = \log_e x$, the distribution is normal if x has a normal distribution but lognormal if y has a normal distribution.

Most economic series probably have an approximately lognormal distribution, as do many series in the physical world. For most economic time series, it is not the variable itself that is characterized by an approximately normal distribution but the first differences in the logs of the variable. The fact that first differences have a normal distribution does not require that their cumulative sum, the series itself (i.e., x or $\log_e x$), also be normal, though they may be.

It is extremely important to clarify the distinctions between these several variables. To do so, we define the four principle variables as follows, where x is the yield to maturity of a particular bond, or the yield of a yield index, such as the Salomon 1-year U.S. government yield index.:

$$y = \log_e x \tag{1}$$
$$\Delta x = x\,(t + 1) - x\,(t) \tag{2}$$
$$\Delta y = y\,(t + 1) - y\,(t) \tag{3}$$
$$= \log_e x\,(t + 1) - \log_e x\,(t)$$

The variable x is the original yield series; y is the natural logarithm of x, (equation [1]); Δx is the first difference in yields (equation [2]); and Δy is the first difference in the natural logarithms of yields (equation [3]). We will be concerned primarily with the difference series; we wish to determine which of them is normal, Δx or Δy. If Δx is normal, we have a normal distribution; if Δy is normal, we have a lognormal distribution. Both Δx and Δy cannot be normal.

A series that has a lognormal distribution is significantly different than a series that has a normal distribution. If changes in yields, Δx, are normally distributed, then the distribution of changes Δx is bell-shaped, symmetrical, and characterized by a standard deviation that is not proportional to the mean change. The expected variation in basis point change in yields is entirely unaffected by the level of yields.

On the other hand in a lognormal distribution, all of the above properties apply but only to changes in the logarithms of yields, or Δy. Changes in the logs of yields will be bell-shaped, symmetrical, and unproportional to the mean. The variability of log changes will be the same for all yield levels.

This lognormality has several consequences. The distribution of changes in yields, where $x = \exp(y)$, is *not* bell-shaped, is *not* symmetrical, and has a standard deviation of changes in yields that is proportional to the level of yields.

We examine the distributions of four variables,—x, Δx, y = $\log_e x$, and Δy—to determine whether they are normal. To examine normality or lognormality, we use Chi-square and tests of skewness and kurtosis. If the distribution of Δx *is* lognormal, we would expect Δy to be normal and Δx not to be normal.

Before making the tests, let's examine a frequency distribution of each of the four variables to see what they look like (see Figure 8.1 A-D). The data are for monthly yields from the Salomon 1-year U.S. government security, January 1950 to June 1986.

The original variable (Graph A) reveals a lack of symmetry, sizable departures from normality, with higher than normal frequencies at the low yields and lower frequencies in

Figure 8.1   Histogram of Yields, Logarithms of Yields, First
Differences in Yields, First Difference in Logarithms of Yields, 1-Year U.S. Bonds, 1950–1986

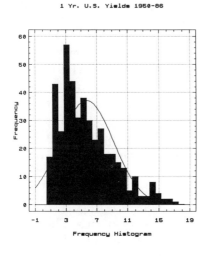

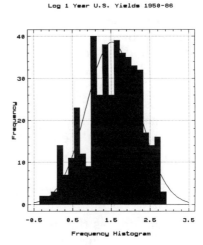

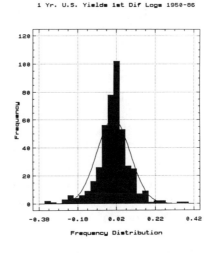

the middle. The distribution is skewed to the right (i.e., it has a long tail in the upper range). If first differences in yields are random, what we have is one realization of the cumulative sums of that process. The first differences in yields (Graph C) are much more like a normal distribution: the distribution is symmetric, and it is not skewed one way or another. Yet the distribution is not completely normal, primarily because there are more observations in the center of the distribution and in the tails than is typical of a normal distribution. There is a corresponding lower number of observations around one standard deviation on either side of the mean. The distribution looks approximately normal, though it would probably not pass a test for normality, based on casual observation.

The logarithms of yields (Graph B) is not symmetric. It has a long tail in the lower yield levels and quite large departures from normality. It clearly cannot be characterized as normal.

The first differences (Graph D) in the logarithms of yields appear to be more normal, though there are departures. The distribution has the usual bell-shaped appearance. The center is peaked, the girth has too few observations, and the tail has more than expected. The distribution is symmetric, approximately normal, but probably not significantly so.

The distributions indicate that neither the yields, nor the logs of yields has a normal distribution. But the first differences, both of yields and of logs of yields, are symmetric. On the basis of the table, however, first differences of both yields and logs of yields look approximately normal. It is not possible to say which is more normal, which less.

We will look at three tests: Chi-square, skewness, and kurtosis. The Chi-square test is based on 20 equal expected frequencies for each distribution, a more powerful test than one based on the deviations in Table 8.1

Chi-square 30 significant at 5% level. Skewness 0 is normal. Kurtosis of 3 is normal

Table 8.1 illustrates that none of the four distributions is normal based on the Chi-square test. Yields are skewed to the

**Table 8.1   Tests of Normality for Yields, 1–Year U.S.
Government Yield Index, 1950–1986 (Salomon)**

	Chi-square	Skewness	Kurtosis
Yield x	1292	.9	.4
Ln Yield $y = \log_e x$	2243	−.4	−.5
1st Dif Yield Δx	2189	−1.2	13.7
1st Dif Ln Yield Δy	2189	−.2	3.3

left and the other series are skewed to the right, first differences in logs least so. The first difference series, with a coefficient of kurtosis (13.7) well in excess of the normal value of 3, is leptokurtic with a high peak and wide tails. All the kurtosis figures differ from the normal value of 3, though the first difference in logs series with a kurtosis of 3.3 is quite close. The means (not shown) of the first difference series are not significantly different than zero at the 5% level of significance, and the numbers of increases and decreases in the yields themselves (x) are not significantly different from what you would expect for a random series (5% level of significance), though there are fewer turning points than normal. This is shown in Chapter 24.

It appears that the first-difference series, Δx and Δy, are approximately normal; both are bell-shaped and symmetric though also leptokurtic. Based on the above tests, we cannot say that one is more normal than another. Plots on probability paper of the data in Table 8.1 are of little help in determining which is more normal. In fact, none of the above is sufficient to state whether we have an approximately normal distribution or an approximately lognormal distribution.

The only exception to the usual tests is that the mean of the original yield series (x) exceeds the median, as it would with a lognormal distribution. The median of x is 5.7 and the mean is 5.0. For the three other distributions, the median exceeds the mean.

Conclusion

We have shown that yields are approximately a lognormal distribution, not a normal distribution. Moreover, the only test that confirmed this conclusion was a test of whether the standard deviation of first differences in yields was directly proportional to the level of yields, as would be the case for a lognormal distribution but not for a normal distribution.

The following is clear from our examination of the distribution of yields and the distribution of changes in yields and their log transforms.

1. The distribution of yields and the logs of yields is not normal.
2. The distribution of changes in yields and changes in the logs of yields is approximately normal.
3. The approximate normality of changes in yields and the logs of yields suggests that the series may be random.

PART **III**

The Mean Change in Yields

The first difference series of the first section suggests that the mean change in interest rates is unpredictable, except in a probability sense. For a stationary random series of normal distribution, we can predict the mean and its probable error. Whether we can make similar predictions for interest rates is another question. In this section we ask whether the mean change is significantly different from zero, and whether zero change is a better predictor of the future than actual past changes are. We also ask whether the standard error, as normally used in statistical analysis, is a good measure of future error. If the answer is no, we have in interest rates a slightly less tractable variable than a pure random number. We also look at the question of whether the proportion of increases in yields is related to the level of yields. If not, interest rates have no normal level about which they fluctuate, but are more a random walk without reflecting barriers.

CHAPTER 9

Is the Mean
Change Significantly
Different from Zero?

W e have shown that the distribution of yields and the distribution of logs of yields are not normal, but that changes in each variable are approximately so. Now we wish to look at a related question, the mean change in yields.

A major issue in the investigation of interest rates is whether rates exhibit a trend. For many economic series, such as common stock prices, there is an upward bias, a positive move over the long-run statistical nature of the average. In these series, each of the components of the average is approximately normally distributed and of zero mean; but the average itself has a positive mean that is a mathematical function of the cross-sectional standard deviation. Stock, commodity, and other arithmetic averages have this upward bias, usually about 5% per year or so. Interest rates, since they are not averages, lack this underlying bias for an upward movement.

Although interest rates lack a statistical reason for rising, they do exhibit a characteristic common to other price series. Namely, they exhibit substantial comovement, much more pronounced than that of stock prices and perhaps than that of commodity prices. There is no reason that the comovement does not cause or lead to any upward movement. In the absence of a reason for upward (or for that matter, downward) movement in interest rates, we can examine the degree to which rates do or do not exhibit statistically significant trends. We will defer to later chapters other kinds of tests on trends, runs, signs, and other tests. (See also Chapters 24, 25, and 26.)

The significance of a mean change may be tested by dividing the mean by the ratio of the standard deviation and the square root of the number of months. This gives us the t-test:

$$t = \frac{\text{mean}}{s\,(n-1)^{.5}}$$

For samples of over 20, the trend, or mean, is significant at the 5% level when t exceeds 1.95. This tests assumes normality of the values of t.

In Tables 9.1 to 9.5, we give the means and the t-tests for various series. Note that the tests covering a single period, such as the tests for all of the U.S. government yield curves in the period 1950 to 1986 (Table 9.2), are really tests of the same data due to the high degree of comovement noted above. The only really long run test of the mean is on the British consol series (Table 9.5), which covers a couple of centuries.

To answer the question of whether the mean is significantly different than zero, we have statistics on the mean change in natural logarithms for the major series we studied. For each series, we take the full span for which we have data. The tables give the mean change in the natural logarithms of the series, the standard deviation of change over the same period, and the T-statistic. If we hypothesize that the mean change is not significantly different than zero and examine the T-value, we will require a T-value of 1.96 or larger to reject the hypothesis. In only one case was the T-value greater than 1.96, as identified by an *. In all other cases, the mean change in the natural logarithms of yields was not significantly different from zero.

**Table 9.1   Corporate Bond Yield Indexes, 1900–1965,
Mean Change in Natural Logarithms**

Maturity	Mean	Standard Deviation	T-Value	n
1-Year	.0007	.254	.02	66
5-Year	.0037	.131	.18	66
10-Year	.0042	.094	.36	66
15-Year	.0042	.077	.44	66
20-Year	.0042	.069	.49	66
25-Year	.0042	.065	.52	66
30-Year	.0042	.063	.54	66

**Table 9.2   Government Bond Yield Indexes, 1950–1986,
Mean Change in Natural Logarithms**

Maturity	Mean	Standard Deviation	T-Value	n
3-Month	.0043	.099	.91	443
6-Month				
1-Year	.0043	.084	1.07	443
2-Year	.0043	.072	1.24	443
5-Year	.0041	.052	1.66	443
10-Year	.0035	.039	1.89	443
20-Year	.0032	.033	2.05[*]	443
30-Year				

[*]T-value greater than 1.96

Table 9.3   Macaulay Yield Indexes, 1857–1937, Monthly, Mean Change in Natural Logarithms

Maturity	Mean	Standard Deviation	T-Value	n
Commercial Paper	–.0026	.117	.68	961
Long-Corporate	–.0010	.021	1.39	957

Table 9.4   Corporate Bond Yield Indexes, Standard & Poor, Monthly, Mean Change in Natural Logarithms

Maturity	Mean	Standard Deviation	T-Value	n
3-Month, 1958–1977	.0035	.088	.062	240
Long-Corp., 1938–1979	.0009	.016	1.69	958

Table 9.5   British Consol Yields, 1730–1961, Annual, Mean Change in Natural Logarithms

Maturity	Mean	Standard Deviation	T-Value	n
Perpetuity	.0027	.067	0.62	232

Quite clearly, for these series in any case, the mean change in yields was not significantly different than zero.

Conclusion

We may conclude the following:

1. The mean change interest rates is not significantly different from zero.
2. The mean change in the logarithms of interest rates is not significantly different from zero.
3. If we wish to forecast the change in interest rates, our best estimate is no change. The most recent interest rate is the best estimate of the next rate.

CHAPTER **10**

The Standard Error
of the Mean

Having looked at the significance of the mean change in interest rates and found it to be not significantly different from zero, we now wish to look at the same question in a slightly different way. We want to look at how means computed in different periods vary from one another and how well the standard error of the mean measures the variability of future means. We will also look at the estimated standard error of the mean in relation to the standard deviation of future means computed over the same length time interval.

More specifically, we will examine the following questions:

1. What have been the mean changes in rates in different periods?
2. Is the standard error of estimate, as normally computed in statistics, a reliable measure of the future error?
3. Does the relationship of the standard deviation to the mean change as we increase the length of the period of change?

We also want to see what kinds of patterns emerge as we go from the means of short periods to the means of long periods. We will begin with an examination of the means and end with summaries of the data.

First we will look at data for the longest series of rates we have. Table 10.1 shows the mean change in British consol yields for 10-year periods beginning in 1730 and ending in 1961. The means are computed the change in the natural logs of yields. Approximate annual percentage changes in yields may be obtained by multiplying by 100, as done in Table 10.1. You can see that there is considerable variation in the means. If we simply chose the mean in one decade as the best estimate of the mean in the next decade, we would be off by a considerable amount, especially since, in this particular set of means, a positive mean in one decade was often followed by a negative mean in the next. Thus, the mean in one decade gives little indication of the mean in the next.

An alternative to simply looking at the mean change is to look at the mean in conjunction with the standard error. The standard error of the mean is computed by dividing the standard deviation of the items used to compute the mean by the square root of the number of items. A fundamental statistical theorem says that two-thirds of the means of the population should lie within one standard error of the mean.

We want to know whether the standard-error rule is true (or, at the very least, useful) for changes in interest rates. We can examine the question by looking at how well a past mean and its standard error portended the future mean. To do so, we will determine whether the future mean lies within the range of the past mean, plus or minus its standard error. Refer to Table 10.2. It is important to understand exactly what we show in Table 10.2 because we will summarize the table in later tables. You will have to understand what is in the core table to appreciate its summaries.

The first column of Table 10.2 is the decade; the second column is the mean change in the natural log of yields; the third column is the standard error of the mean $(s/n^{.5})$; the fourth column is the past mean minus one standard error, the

**Table 10.1   Changes in Logs of British Consol Yields,
1730–1961, Mean 10-Year Changes in the Logs of
Yields, Nonoverlapping Decades, 1730–1961**

Decade	x100
1730-1740	-.9
1740-1750	0
1750-1760	2.3
1760-1770	-0.3
1770-1780	2.9
1780-1790	-2.2
1790-1800	1.9
1800-1810	-.5
1810-1820	-.1
1820-1830	-2.4
1830-1840	-.4
1840-1850	-.7
1850-1860	.2
1860-1870	.2
1870-1880	-.6
1880-1890	-1.3
1890-1900	0
1900-1910	1.4
1910-1920	5.5
1920-1930	-1.8
1930-1940	-2.7
1940-1950	-.4
1950-1960	4.2

fifth column is the past mean plus one standard error, and the sixth column is the number of future means within one standard error of the present mean. The figures have been multiplied by 100 to make them more comprehensible. The resulting figures are roughly equal to the annual percentage change in yields. As you can see, each row pertains to a particular decade.

Table 10.2   Change in Log of British Consol Yields, 1730–1961

Period	Mean*	Standard Error*	Mean −SE*	Mean +SE*	Percent within 1 SE of Past Mean
(1)	(2)	(3)	(4)	(5)	(6)
1730–1740	− .9	1.6	−2.5	.6	68%
1740–1750	0	2.2	−2.2	2.2	71
1750–1760	2.3	1.7	− .6	4.0	15
1760–1770	− .3	3.0	−3.4	2.6	84
1770–1780	2.9	2.1	.8	5.1	17
1780–1790	−2.2	2.7	−5.0	.5	76
1790–1800	1.9	3.8	−1.9	5.6	88
1800–1810	− .5	2.7	−3.2	2.2	87
1810–1820	− .1	3.1	−3.2	3.0	86
1820–1830	−2.4	2.2	−4.6	− .1	46
1830–1840	− .4	1.2	−1.6	.8	58
1840–1850	− .7	1.5	−2.3	.8	64
1850–1860	.2	1.0	−.8	1.3	40
1860–1870	.2	.7	−.6	.9	33
1870–1880	−.6	.2	−.9	− .3	0
1880–1890	−1.3	.7	−2.1	− .6	14
1890–1900	0	1.6	−1.6	1.6	33
1900–1910	1.4	.8	.7	2.2	0
1910–1920	5.5	1.7	3.8	7.2	25
1920–1930	−1.8	1.7	−3.5	− 0	33
1930–1940	−2.7	3.0	−5.7	.3	0
1940–1950	− .4	2.6	−2.1	3.0	0
1950–1960	4.2	2.4	1.8	6.6	—
Average	2.0	1.9			54

*All figures x100.

The standard error of the mean was computed by calculating the standard deviation of the 10 changes used to calculate the annual change over the decade and then dividing that standard deviation by the square root of 10 (or, by 3.16). If the mean change in rates during the decade 1910 to 1920 was an accurate measure of the future, then the future means, those in the next four decades, should lie within that range. The last column shows what proportion of the future means lay within one standard error of that decade's mean. We determined this by counting the number of future means (column 2) that lay within one standard error of the decade mean, i.e. within the boundaries of columns 4 and 5.

The 2.0 is the standard deviation of the means, i.e. the standard deviation of the figures in the column above.

If you look at the row 1910-1920, you will see that the mean and its standard error predicted only one of the means of the next four decades which is a rate of 25%. The 25% is entered on the far right, in column 6, for the period 1910-1920.

Twenty-five percent is not what we would expect. A more reasonable figure is 68%, assuming things don't change from one decade to the next. But you can see by going down column 6, the percentage was 68% or above 7 of 22 years. In the remaining 15 years, the percent was below the expected value. The average percent was 54%, as shown at the bottom of column 6. Table 10.2 provides a test of how well the standard error and the past mean actually do predict the future. Quite clearly, the success rate is low.

Look again at the individual percentages in Column 6. You can see how much the accuracy of the mean and standard error vary in estimating future means. In a couple of cases, all future means were outside the range predicted. In a few others, 80% to 90% were within the range. This wide variance in accuracy is due both to the variability of the standard error and to the variability of the mean. Aside from the fact that larger standard errors give better forecast results, there doesn't seem to be much pattern.

Table 10.2 presents data for 10 year periods and has an average percent within one standard error of 54%. We can also look at the average percent within one standard error for other time periods, such as 2, 3, 4, 5, and up to 20 years for this data.

Table 10.3 summarizes these data.

Column 1 is the number of years of changes in the logs of interest rates used to compute the other figures.

Column 2 is the standard deviation of the means. For the ten year period, it is the standard deviation of column 2 of Table 10.2.

Column 3 is the mean of the estimated standard errors. For the ten year period, it is the mean of column 3 of Table 10.2.

Column 4 is the mean of the standard deviations (not shown but used in deriving the standard errors).

Column 5 is the percent of the time that the actual future means were within the standard error of the prior mean. This figure should be 68%, but as you can see, it is generally far lower. The median is about 50%, so the standard error substantially underestimates the actual standard deviation of the future means. Since we use the same future data over and over again, the items in column 6 are not independent of each other.

According to the law of large numbers, as we increase the sample size, the mean should move closer and closer to the true mean. In Table 10.3, we increase the sample size as we increase the number of years over which we calculate the mean. The number of years increases from 1 year to 23 years. Consequently, the variability of the mean, the standard deviation of the means, and the standard error of the means should all decrease. We can see that they do decrease.

The final conclusion to be drawn from Table 10.3 is that the actual standard deviation of the means and the estimated standard error of the means should be the same, but they are not. (The actual standard deviation is given in column 2, and the estimated standard error appears in column 3.) For shorter periods, nine years or less, the actual standard deviation is considerably higher. As the length of the period increases, the estimated standard error rises. It is unknown why this is true.

Table 10.3   Changes in Logs of British Consol Yields, 1730–1961, Average Statistics for Different Length Periods

Num- ber of Years	Standard Deviation of Means*	Mean of Standard Errors*	Mean of Standard Deviation*	Future Means within 1 Std. Error (%)*	Number of Means
(1)	(2)	(3)	(4)	(5)	(6)
1	6.7	—	—	—	232
2	5.4	2.8	4.0	27	116
3	3.9	3.1	5.3	42	77
4	3.7	2.7	5.4	40	58
5	3.0	2.6	5.8	46	46
6	3.0	2.3	5.7	42	38
7	2.6	2.3	6.0	51	33
8	2.4	2.1	6.0	47	29
9	2.3	2.0	6.1	52	25
10	2.0	1.9	6.2	54	23
11	1.9	1.9	6.0	62	21
12	2.1	1.7	6.0	47	19
13	1.5	1.7	6.1	57	17
14	1.4	1.6	6.1	57	16
15	1.4	1.6	6.2	55	15
16	1.1	1.6	6.2	67	14
17	1.5	1.5	6.1	51	13
18	1.6	1.4	6.0	45	12
19	1.5	1.4	6.2	48	12
20	1.0	1.4	6.2	69	11
21	1.7	1.3	6.2	36	11
22	1.1	1.3	6.2	62	10
23	1.1	1.3	6.2	49	10

*All figures x100.

The Graphical Evidence

We can look at the same data more clearly by examining graphs of changes in interest rates. Figure 10.1 shows the mean change in rates for selected time periods. We will examine these figures to determine that the mean varies significantly from one period to the next, that the mean in any period is not necessarily a good indication of the mean in the next, and finally, that the mean declines in absolute value with an increase in the number of months or years over which it is measured. These conclusions will reinforce what we have learned already.

Graph A of Figure 10.1 shows the annual change in the logs of interest rates for 23 nonoverlapping decades between 1730 and 1961 (British consol data). The length of this period, coupled with the fact that this is an actual yield series, not an index, gives it much credibility. Scan the graph from left to right. You can see that it would be very difficult to estimate the next decade change in yields from the last, not only in predicting whether the next decade change would be positive or negative but in predicting the. magnitude of the change, as well. In the first decade, the mean was negative; in the next zero; in the third positive. The next four decades alternate between falls and rises in the mean. Then there are five successive decades of decline, followed by zero, and then alternating double decades of rises and falls for six decades in succession. Here is a list of just the increases and decreases in this series:

- .. + - + - + - - - - - + + - - + + - - + +

Clearly, there is very little pattern to the means, just as there was very little pattern to the individual month or year changes we found earlier. The result of averaging does not appear to be a rise in regularity of positive and negative changes. We seem to have the same randomness, the same apparent chaos, we had before. Now look at the magnitude of changes to see if that provides any pattern. During the first nine decades, the eighteenth and early nineteenth centuries, there were changes of high magnitude every other decade or so. Then in the mid- and latter nineteenth century, the degree of change suddenly lessened. No longer were the mean changes so great. Finally, in the twentieth century, the magnitude of change became large again, larger than in any period since the eighteenth and early nineteenth centuries.

In Tables 10.1, 10.2, and 10.3, we saw that the past mean and its standard error were not very good purveyors of the future mean. At least half the time, the future mean did not lie between the past mean and its standard error. This was contrary to the theory that the future mean should be within one standard error of the past mean, unless, of course, things had changed and the series was not invariant over time.

Figure 10.1 illustrates that this would be the case, that the past mean and its standard error (not shown) might not be very good indicators of the future mean. The sharp changes in the mean itself suggest this. In fact, you might be able to guess from the figure that only half the future estimates would be within one error because past means would be too high (too positive) or too low (too negative) to reasonably reflect what the future mean might be. We might suspect that a mean of zero might give a better estimate of the future mean.

To be sure that the data for the British consols is not invalid, let's look at some other data. The other graphs of Figure 10.1 present data from three additional series-long corporate yields, 1900 to 1979; commercial paper yields, 1857 to 1937; long corporate yields, 1857 to 1936; 3-month U.S. yields, 1950 to 1986, and 20-year U.S. yields, 1950 to 1956. The figures are drawn to different scales, so the magnitudes are not comparable. But by comparing the five new graphs (A, B, C, D, and E) with the consol graph (A), you can see that the random character of the data does not change.

In sum, it would be difficult to estimate future means from past means. The main exception might be the long corporates, 1957 to 1936, where yields were down for eight of nine decades in succession, but then suddenly the series changed.

Figure 10.1 Average Annual Changes in Yields, Selected Series

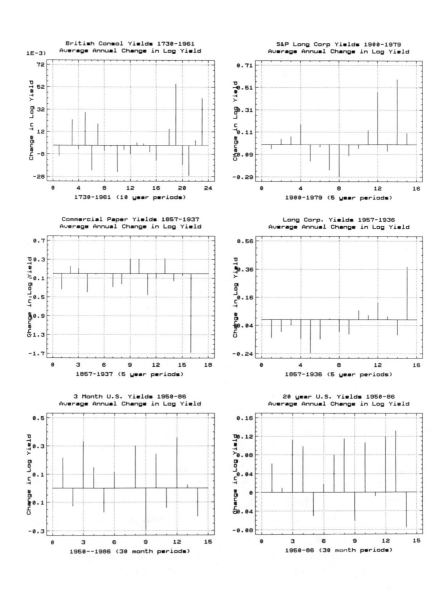

We have seen the difficulty of predicting the mean, either in direction or magnitude. Now, we turn to a different aspect of the mean that it is possible to predict with considerable accuracy, as illustrates shown in the next figures. Figure 10.2 illustrates four different time periods - 1, 4, 9, and 16 years - using British consol data. In Figure 10.2, all of the data are drawn on the same scale, so the actual mean is shown.

You can observe several significant characteristics. First, as we increase the period over which the mean is calculated, the apparent randomness of the mean does not change either in direction or magnitude. That is, the past doesn't give much indication as to whether the next mean will be up or down or what its magnitude will be relative to past changes. This is similar to what we found in the earlier figures.

But one feature is very pronounced: The average absolute mean change declines markedly with an increase in the difference interval, i.e. the interval over which we compute the mean change. For the 1-year period, the mean change frequently exceeded 0.15, up or down. In the 4-year period, the change never attained an absolute value of 0.15 and was generally below 0.05. In the 9-year period, the mean change exceeded 0.05 only twice and was generally below 0.02. In the 16-year period, the mean change was generally below 0.02 in absolute value. Figure 10.4 shows this very clearly.

By observing the same figure, we can infer that the standard deviation of *means* of changes in the logs of rates will decline with an increase in the time interval over which the change is measured. Although we don't show the standard deviations on Figure 10.2, you can see that it will decline with the drop in the mean changes. Certainly, if the degree of change in the means declines, the standard deviations will decline as well, by definition.

We test this conclusion directly in Figure 10.3, which shows the standard deviation of the means of changes in the logs of yields for four series. In Graph A, the means of changes in commercial paper yields are shown as a function of the number of months of data used to calculate the means. The number of months in each mean rises from 1 to 94. The stand-

Figure 10.2 1-Year, 4-Year, 9-Year, and 16-Year Mean Annual Change in Consol Yields, 1730–1961

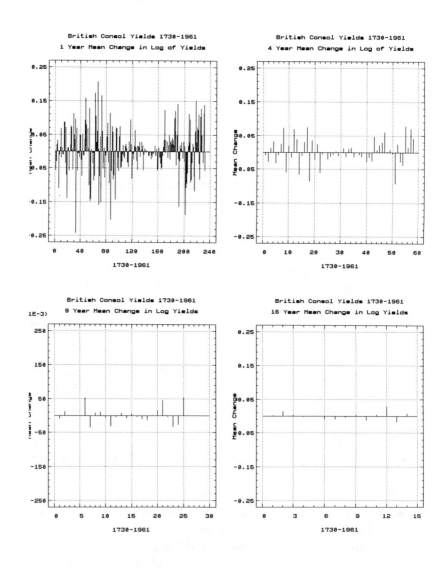

Figure 10.3 Standard Deviation of Mean Change in Yields Versus Number of Months Used in Calculating Mean, Various Series, Log Log Scale

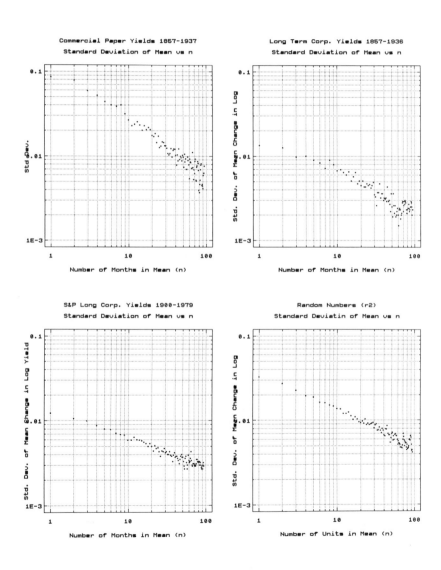

Figure 10.4 Standard Deviation of Mean Change in Yields Versus Number of Months Used in Calculating Mean, Various Series, Arithmetic Scale

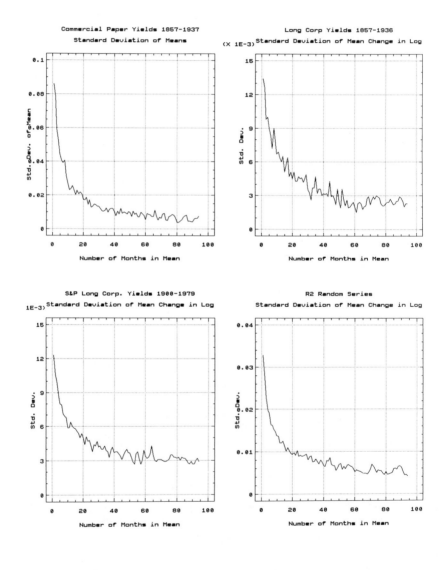

ard deviation of the means is calculated using nonoverlapping intervals. We would expect the standard deviation to decline with the square root of n. That rate of decline would appear as a downward sloping line with a slope of 0.5 on a log log chart. (A log log chart uses a log scale in both axes).

Figure 10.3 gives data for long-term yields in two periods, 1857 to 1936 and 1900 to 1979, and also for a random series ($r2$). All of the slopes are negative, all are roughly 0.5, and the pattern is consistent in all cases. The commercial paper has a more pronounced downward slope than the other series.

An alternative presentation of the same data is given in Figure 10.4 which shows the standard deviation of the means versus n but this time on a line arithmetic scale. Here, the relationship is not linear, since we don't use a log log chart, but you can see the downward movement. As in Figure 10.3, the calculation is based on nonoverlapping periods. Because the periods don't overlap, we pick up different end-points and, hence, variability in s.

Conclusion

Based on our analysis in this chapter, we can conclude that the following are the principal characteristics of the mean change in the logs of interest rates where n is the number of units of time used to calculate the mean:

1. Past and future mean changes in yield show a great deal of variability.

2. The longer the period over which the mean is calculated (the more months or years used, n), the less the degree of variability in the means. The variability of the means declines with n.

3. The standard deviation of the means of changes in the logs of yields declines with the number of months used in calculating the means.

4. The average standard error of the means declines with the square root of n ($s/n^{.5}$).

CHAPTER 11

Forecasting the Future Mean from the Past Mean and Its Standard Error

The standard error of the mean, s_{avg}, is frequently used to gauge the reliability of the past mean in predicting the future. This measure of reliability depends on how well s gauges the long-run variability. For any number of reasons, s may not be a good measure of the future nor may the past mean.

This chapter is a continuation of the questions raised in the previous chapter. However, in this chapter, we will investigate the standard error of the mean and the accuracy of using the standard error to estimate the range of future changes in interest rates. We will further examine whether it is better to use zero as the best estimate of future changes in rates or to use actual past means. Our method of investigation will be to determine whether more future means are within one standard error when we base our estimate on zero or when we base it on actual past means. If we have a set of independent variables $x_1, x_2, \ldots, x_n$, with identical means, m, and variances, s^2, where their average is:

$$x(avg) = (1/n) (x_1 + x_2 + \ldots + x_{n)} \text{ Then}$$

then

$$\text{mean } x = m$$

and

$$s^2_{x \text{ (avg)}} = s^2/n$$
$$s_{x \text{ (avg)}} = s/n^{.5}$$

That means that the variance of the means declines with n and the standard deviation declines with the square root of n.

The standard deviation shrinks as we increase n. When we turn to interest rates and consider the effect of increasing the interval over which we measure the mean and variance, we in effect are increasing the sample size, increasing n. Thus, if we take the mean of 48 monthly changes in rates and compare it to the mean of a 12 monthly changes in rates, we have four times as many monthly changes. Consequently, the variance of the 48 monthly changes should be only one-fourth as large as the variance of the 12 monthly changes. Since the standard deviation is the square root of the variance, the standard deviation of the 48 monthly changes should be only half as large as the standard deviation of the 12 monthly changes. That is to say: the variance will decline with n and the standard deviation will decline with the square root of n. This has several consequences:

1. The mean expected value is independent of n.
2. The standard deviation of the mean will decline with the square root of n. In other words, the more trials we make, the smaller the divergence between the mean values of those trials and the expected mean.
3. If we plotted the standard deviation of the mean against n on log log paper, we would get a line sloping downward to the right with a slope of one half.
4. The standard error of the mean should be the standard deviation of the n items used to compute the mean divided by the square root of n. This is a corollary of (2) above.
5. If we compare the estimated standard error of the mean with the actual standard deviation of a set of means, the two figures should coincide.

Our next problem is to determine whether the standard error, as defined above and as normally calculated in statistics, is really a good measure of the error for an interest rate series. We will compute means for selected nonoverlapping segments of changes in yields, find their standard deviation, determine the standard error of these means, and then compare the expected standard error of the means with the actual standard deviation of the means. When after we've made the calculations, we will chart them to clarify the comparison.

Graph A of Figure 11.1 shows the actual standard deviation of a set of means of a set of random numbers together with the mean standard error of those means. For this random series, the standard deviation is computed from the means. A standard error is computed for each mean and the set of standard errors is averaged. To make the computation, we begin with means of two items and then continue through 3, 4, 5, and up to n items. The first figure is for changes in the logs of a random series that was constructed to emulate interest rates.

Graph A of Figure 11.1 illustrates two things:

1. The standard deviation, and with it the standard error, decline as n increases. This is what we would expect if s and SE are related to $1/n^5$.

2. There is a close correspondence between the actual standard deviations of the means and the estimated standard errors. Again, this is what we would expect. The actual standard deviation is a little more volatile when n is large, primarily because of declining sample size.

Next, let's look at the same kind of figure for actual interest rates. Graphs B, C, and D of Figure 11.1 presents the same information for long bonds, 1900-1979; commercial paper 1857 to 1937; and long bonds 1857 to 1936. The three interest-rate series show the same decline in s with n and also the same tendency of the actual standard deviation of the means to be larger than the estimated standard error.

Figure 11.1   Standard Deviation of Means and Estimated Standard Error of Mean Versus Number of Month Used in Calculating the Mean Various Series

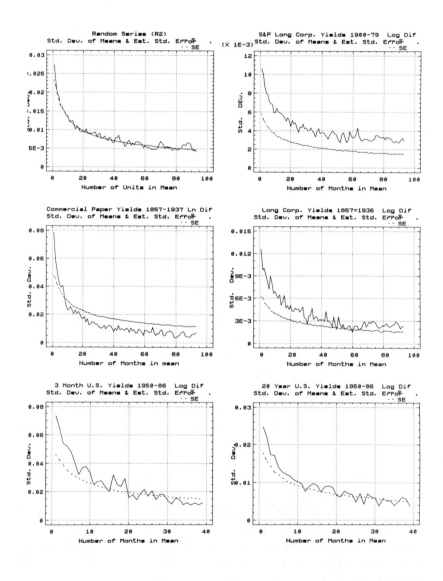

Not only that, but for the two long-bond series, the standard deviation is consistently larger than the standard error, substantially so in the case of the S&P long-bond series from 1900 to 1979. Why this disparity exists is not known. But it does reveal that the normal procedure for estimating the standard error for changes in the logs of interest rates produces an estimate that is too low.

Graphs E and F of Figure 11.1 give the same data for U.S. government yields from 1950 to 1986, and we find the same kind of characteristics. We can make the following observations:

1. Both the standard deviation and the standard error decline with n. This is what we found in the previous chapter where we plotted figures on a log log chart of s against n (Figure 10.3).

2. The standard deviation and the estimated standard error are no longer the same. When n is small— under twenty for 3-month bills and under twenty for 1-, 2-, and 20-year bonds—the actual standard deviation is considerably higher than the standard error. This is indeed surprising. Thereafter, the standard error tends to exceed the standard deviation, which is not what we might expect. We might wonder whether this is true of other time periods and other types of securities.

Figure 11.2 gives the ratio of the actual standard deviation to the estimated standard error for the interest rate series described above. As you can see, the standard deviation ranges from 1.5 times the standard error to 2.0 times as much for shorter periods and less for longer periods.

The main conclusion to be drawn upon reviewing these figures is that you can't simply compute the mean and standard error of past changes in interest rates and expect two-thirds of the future means to fall within one standard error. The standard deviation of actual means of interest rate changes is generally higher, particularly for short periods, than the

Figure 11.2 Standard Deviation of Means/Estimated Standard Error of Mean Versus Number of Month Used in Calculating the Mean, Various Series

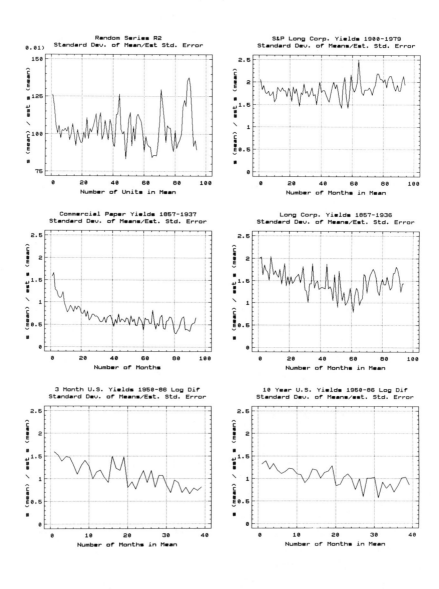

estimated standard error. In other words, the estimated standard error is an underestimate; it's too low for some series for smaller n, for under a year or two of monthly data, and for other series, as well. Evidently, to produce a better estimate, we must increase the standard estimate of the mean by a factor of 1.5 or more.

Having discussed this, we may now ask, what is the accuracy of using the past mean and the standard error of estimate to forecast future means? More specifically, if we were to use the past mean and its standard error to decide on the range of future means, what percentage of the future means would fall within one standard error? Would it be 68% as expected, or, would it be less? Also, in asking the above question, would we be better off using a zero mean instead of the past actual mean? In other words, do we get a better forecast of the future mean change by saying the mean change will be zero?

Although asking this final question does not give us a statistical test of the mean, it does give us a quite pragmatic sense of the answer. It tells whether the mean is more likely to be zero than some other number. If we get better results using zero, we have an indication that the future mean change in the logs of rates is more probably zero than any actual figure we might derive from a sample of past data.

Figure 11.3 shows the percentage of future means that were within the past mean and plus or minus one standard error for the British consol yields. The data are as calculated in Chapter 10. The expected value is 68%, but it was not 68% during most of the periods. For periods of less than eight years, the value was below 50%. Only rarely was it above 68%. We might expect this result based on our previous look at the standard error, where we found the standard error underestimated the standard deviation, particularly for shorter periods.

Instead of using the past mean as our guide to the future, we can use a zero mean and then examine how many future mean changes in the logs of yields lie within one standard

Figure 11.3 Future Means Within 1 Standard Error of Zero Mean, Actual Past Mean, Various Yield Series

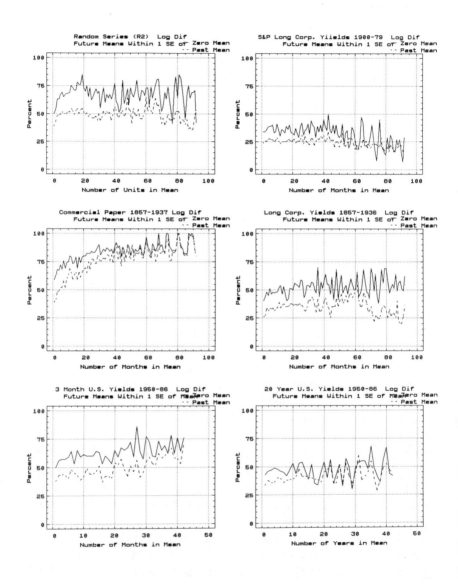

error of zero. We can compare those results with the results we get using actual past means. The effects are also given in the graphs of Figure 11.3 which show the results of both methods. Note that the zero mean gives better results. Graph A of Figure 11.3 shows the same data for the random series. In most cases, the zero mean provides a better result, even for the random series.

Conclusion

1. The estimated standard error underestimates the standard deviation of the mean change in the logs of interest rates.
2. Zero change is better than the past mean at estimating future changes in the logs of interest rates.
3. The standard error underestimates the proportion of future means that will lie within one standard error of the mean (whether zero or past actual).
4. The normal procedure of estimating the standard error cannot be applied to interest rates since such estimates are too low.

CHAPTER **12**

Does the Level of Yields Affect the Frequency of Increases or Decreases in Yields?

It is natural to suppose that, when interest rates are high, yields are more likely to drop, and when interest rates are low, yields are more likely to rise? If you ask a professional investment manager whether this is true, he or she is quite likely to say that it is. The same answer is likely to be given by the average investor, the economist at the bank,—in fact, by practically anyone you ask. To think otherwise seems contrary to both intuition and logic and, it might be added, to common, everyday experience. When things are high, they tend to drop, and vice versa.

What seems obvious is not necessarily so, however. In the case of interest rates, it is not easy to assess what is high and what is low. In the 1950s a 3% interest rate may have seemed high, but in the 1980s 3% is extraordinarily low. Likewise, the 1950s 13% may have seemed out of the question, but by mid-1980s 13% was to many a sort of watershed that would likely again be exceeded. Our view of what is high and low will always be colored by recent experience. In fact, the more recent, the more relevant, it seems.

If we look at changes in interest rates as a random process, the question naturally arises as to whether the movements are subject to what physicists call *reflecting barriers*. Consider this example: If a visible gas is released in the air, and it is lighter than air at the surface of the earth, it will disperse, and some of its particles will rise. At a certain elevation, however, the gas molecules may become lighter than the surrounding air; at that level, the molecules will have a greater tendency to bounce back to lower elevations than to rise. This certain elevation acts as a reflecting barrier, forming a boundary to the diffusion of the gas.

The same thing may happen to interest rates. That boundary condition—the reflecting barrier—is what leads individuals to assume that rates that are high will have a tendency to fall.

This boundary condition can also be viewed as a tendency to revert to the mean, a capacity of rates to return to some normal value. In nature a large number of phenomena do revert to a mean. The daily temperature, for example, rises during daylight hours and falls at night, in response to the effect of the 24-hour rotation of the earth. The temperature in Minnesota rises in the summer and falls in the winter, reverting in each extreme season to some kind of annual mean. In both cases of these natural phenomena, there is clear evidence of a mean-reverting tendency, of reflections at the boundary, and also of an observable cause associated with the cyclical behavior.

In the case of interest rates, the situation is not so easily observable or so arguable. Although we may think that the minimum rate on money is zero, that is not the lower boundary, since for a bank account with charges and no interest, the rate is negative. Nor is there any clear upper boundary, for in certain times, rates rise to 50%, 100%, or even 200% per annum, many-fold the usual rate.

We will examine this issue by looking at the actual frequencies of increases in rates for various levels of rates in order to see whether there really is an observably higher proportion of increases when rates are low (for that particular series) and a lower proportion of increases when rates are high. This then is a straightforward historical examination of the issue. If there is a marked tendency for rates to rise more often in periods of low rates and vice versa, then the data should show this. If they do not, we can conclude that there is no mean-reverting tendency in interest rates and there are no reflecting barriers.

Let's look at the data. The graphs in Figure 12.1 have been arranged so that for each level of yield, (0.0%-0.9%, 1.0%-1.9%, etc. up to 16.0%-16.9%), we can observe the percentage of times in which the yield increased. The proportion of increases is computed as the ratio of times in which yields increased to the total number of changes. In order to ensure that the sample at each yield level was sufficiently large, only those cases where there were at least 10 changes have been included.

Figure 12.1 covers the period of 1950 to 1986 for six different yield indexes. Look carefully at the figure. Note that there is no marked tendency for the proportion of increases to decline as the beginning yield rises. The dots are scattered across the page, generally in the same range. Most of the time, the proportion of increases in yields ranges from 40% to 60%. Very careful scrutiny of the graphs will reveal that, for these series, when yields were in the lower ranges, the proportion of increases exceeded 50%, but when the yields were in the upper ranges, the proportion of increases was sometimes above and sometimes below 50%. The tendency does not appear to be strong enough to be statistically significant, however.

Table 12.1 shows the proportion of increases for this series. By examining the table you can see whether there is any relationship between the proportion of increases and the beginning yield in the 3-month bond. It is clear that the proportion of increases was just about as high when yields were high as when yields were low. When yields were 9%, for example, yields increased 58% of the time the following month. When yields were 1%, they increased 57% of the time.

Figure 12.1 Frequency of Increases in Yields Versus Beginning Yield, U.S. Government Bonds, 1950–1986

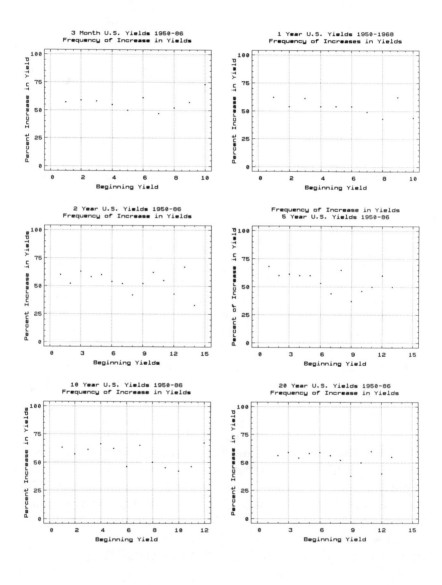

Table 12.1   Proportion of Increases in Yields by Beginning Yield U.S. Yield Yields, 1950–1986 (Salomon)

Beginning Yield	1/3	1	2	5	10	20
			Maturity in Years			
			Proportion of Increases			
1	57	62	60	68		
2	59	54	52	60	63	56
3	58	61	63	61	57	59
4	55	54	58	60	61	54
5	50	54	60	60	66	58
6	61	54	54	53	62	59
7	47	49	52	44	46	56
8	52	43	42	65	65	52
9	58	62	52	37	50	
10	73	44	62	46	45	50
11			55	50	42	60
12				60	46	40
13				50	67	55
14			33			
F-Value	0.4	4.0	6.0**	4.5	2.1	2.6
R-square	.05	.33	.37**	.29**	.18	.23
Beta	+	—	—	—	—	—

**Significant F-Statistic or R square for regression of percent of increases on beginning yield.

Excludes samples <10.

Only for the 2-year bonds was there a significant relationship between beginning yields and subsequent changes in yields.

Tables 12.1 and 12.2 show not only the proportion of increases for various beginning yields (where the sample exceeded 9 cases) but also the sign of the relationship, the F-value for the regression, and the coefficient of determination. The beta gives the sign of the relationship. Thus there was an inverse relationship between beginning yield and the frequency of increases in six instances and a direct relationship in three. If there is direct relationship, the higher the beginning yield, the greater the frequency of increases. This just is the reverse of what we might expect if indeed there were a relationship between level of yield and frequency of increases in yield. If you examine the F-values, only two are significant at the 0.05 level. And of those two, one has a positive slope, the other a negative slope.

We can also conduct a signs test for trend using the Cox and Stuart procedure. In doing this test, we divide the sample of frequencies of increase in half and look to see whether the frequencies of increase for the lower beginning yields are higher than the frequencies of increase for the higher yields. In essence, this is a one-sample use of the signs, test and it is a test for trend. In all but one case (the 5-year U.S. government yields) there appears to be no significant evidence of trend. These tests support the regression indicted above.

Conclusion

1. There appears to be no general tendency for the frequency of yields to rise when yields are low, or vice versa.

2. Low yields are not much more likely to rise than are high yields.

3. Similarly, high yields are not much more likely to fall than are low yields.

4. There isn't much tendency in yields to move toward a mean value as evidenced by the proportion of increases or decreases at various yield levels.

Table 12.2   Proportion of Increases in Yield by Beginning Yield

Beginning Yield	Macaulay 1867–1936/7 Comm. Paper	Long-Term	S&P Long 1900–1957	British Consol 1730–1961
0	0			
1	16			
2	39		57	55
3	51	41	57	50
4	50	44	58	54
5	48	44	49	23
6	43	34	36	
7	47	42	60	
8	31	40		
9	47	26		
10	39			
F-Value	3.3	0.7	17.1**	n.a.
R-square	.27	.12	.74**	n.a.
Beta	+	−	+	

[**]Significant F-Statistic or R square for regression of percent of increases on beginning yield.

Excludes samples <10.

5. In general, the frequency of increase or decrease in yields appears to be unrelated to the level of yields.

PART IV

The Dispersion of Interest Rates

An important property of the random walk is that dispersion, measured by the standard deviation, rises with time, or with the difference interval or holding period. The previous sections gave no inkling of the rise of dispersion since their analysis was restricted to the smallest unit of measurement, a month for most of our series. As we expand the difference to 2, 3,..., n months, the standard deviation rises with the square root of n for a random series. That the square root relationship applies to interest rates forms important evidence for the random character of interest rates. We also look at the effect of maturity on volatility and at whether the volatility of interest rates changes from one historical period to another.

CHAPTER **13**

The Standard Deviation of Changes in the Logarithms of Interest Rates Rises with the Difference Interval

In this chapter, we examine next how the standard deviation of changes in the logs of bond yields rises with the difference interval. The *difference interval*, also called the *holding period*, is the time interval over which the change in yields is measured.

The standard deviation measures the degree of change when the direction of change is neglected. When the standard deviation is high, there is greater change and more uncertainty about future rates. When the standard deviation is low, that is not the case.

Our purpose now is to show that there is a systematic relationship between the standard deviation and the difference interval. If there is a relationship and if we know the projected holding period of the bond, plus the maturity as we show later, we can predict future volatility. We want to examine the relationship between two quantities: (1) the variability of changes in interest rates and (2) the difference interval over which the change in rates changes are calculated. We want to see how variability changes as we change the length of the difference interval. Although this relationship is extremely important to time series analysis, it is rarely examined and not often discussed, though for some things, such as option pricing, the theoretical relationship that characterizes random data is assumed.

The theoretical relationship states that variance (s^2) rises with the difference interval. Double the difference interval and variance doubles. Quadruple the difference interval and the variance quadruples. This relationship of variance to the difference interval (t) is the relationship that prevails for random walks. If we take the square root of the variance (s) and the square root of the difference interval ($t^{.5}$), we have the same relationship, but now expressed in terms of the standard deviation. The standard deviation rises with the square root of the difference interval, or with $t^{.5}$.

To examine this relationship for changes in the logarithms of interest rates, we use the following procedure and the following definitions. The difference interval is the length of the period over which the difference in interest rates is measured. If we have daily data, we can compute differences in yields over 1-day intervals, 2-day intervals, and so on. If we have monthly data, we can compute differences over 1-month intervals, 2-month intervals and so on. What we might expect from general observation of interest rates is that the longer the difference interval, the greater the change in rates, up or down. Rates can change more in a month than in a day, more in a year than in a month.

Figure 13.1 shows how the rise in amount of change in rates corresponds to the rise in the difference interval. There are six graphs in Figure 13.1, each portraying changes in interest rates over different length intervals. The interest rates are long bond yields 1857 to 1936. Graph A of Figure 13.1 shows 1-month changes in the logarithms of yields; Graph B shows 4-month changes; Graph C shows 9-month changes; Graph D shows 16-month changes; Graph E shows 25 month changes; and Graph F shows 36-month changes. All of the graphs are drawn to the same scale on the y axis so the degrees of change can be compared with one another.

Figure 13.1 Differences in Logarithms of Yields Versus Difference Interval, Long-Term Bonds, 1857–1936

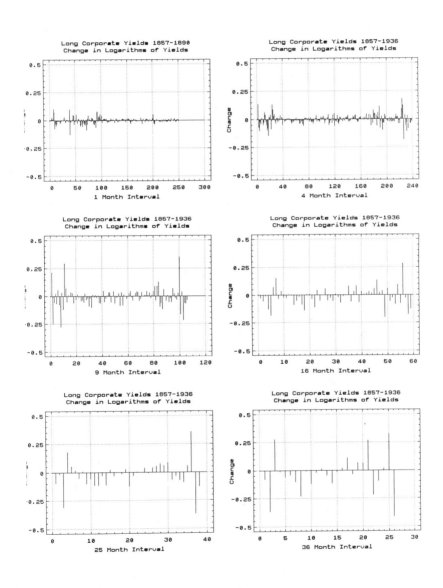

Graph A of Figure 13.1 where the difference interval is 1 month shows smaller changes than Graph B where the difference interval is 4 months. Graph D, where the difference interval is 16 months, shows larger changes than Graph B or Graph A, and smaller changes than Graph E or F. Figure 13.1 demonstrates how the degree of change in interest rates rises as we increase the difference interval.

A more concise way of showing this relationship is to compute the standard deviation of changes in the logarithms of interest rates. That is done in Table 13.1. In this table, we computed the standard deviation of changes in the natural logarithms of interest rates, or for the data shown in Figure 13.1. Note that Graph A of Figure 13.1 does not show all of the monthly changes due to space limitations.

Table 13.1   Difference Interval and Standard Deviation of Changes in the Logarithms of Interest Rates, Long Bond Yields 1857–1936

Data in Figure 13.1	Difference Interval Months	Standard Deviation
(1)	(2)	(3)
Graph A	1	.019
Graph B	4	.039
Graph C	9	.080
Graph D	16	.081
Graph E	25	.118
Graph F	36	.169

The standard deviation shown in Column 3 of Table 13.1 rises with the rise in the difference interval in Column 2.

We can plot the results of these calculations on a log log scale. If the square root holds and we plot the difference interval on the x axis and the standard deviation on the y axis, the dots will form a line extending up to the right with a slope of 0.5.

Graphs so constructed are given in Figure 13.2. To construct Figure 13.2 where the data was monthly, we compute 1-month changes in the natural logarithms of yields and then calculate the standard deviation of these monthly changes. Next, we compute 2-month changes in the same series and again calculate the standard deviation of these changes. Next, we compute 3-month changes and calculate the standard deviation of these changes, and so on. The result of these calculations is a series of standard deviations, s, for the series of difference intervals of $t = 1, 2$, and on up to n months.

Having produced a series of standard deviations for increasing intervals, we wish to determine whether there is any systematic relationship between the series of standard deviations, s, and the series of difference intervals, t. To compute s, we use overlapping intervals. For example, to find s for 2-month intervals, we use all combinations of 2-month intervals in the series. The standard deviation for each difference interval computed using overlapping data is unlike Figure 13.1 above where nonoverlapping data was used. The effect of using overlapping data is to smooth the values of s and the plots. Had we used nonoverlapping intervals, the plots shown in the figures would be much less regular.

Before turning to standard deviations of actual interest rates, we wish to examine the relationship between the standard deviation of changes in the series and the difference interval for a random series. For a random series, we would expect s to rise with the square root of the difference interval. If we plotted s on the y axis of an xy figure and the difference interval on the x axis and used a log log figure, we would expect the scatter points to rise in a straight line with a slope of one-half. This is the nature of stochastic processes, such as coin-flipping experiments and other forms of Brownian motion.

Figure 13.2 Standard Deviation of Differences in Logarithms of Yields Versus Difference Interval, Selected Yield Series

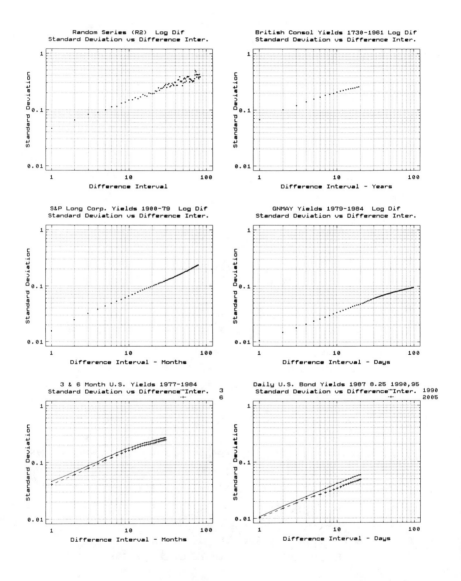

Table 13.2 Standard Deviation of Differences in Logs of
Yields Versus Length of the Difference Interval—
Monthly, Macaulay and Random Number
Series R2, Bond Yields 1857-1937

Difference Interval Months	Commercial Paper	Long-Term Corporate Bonds	Random Numbers R2
(1)	(2)	(3)	(4)
1	.12	.02	.05
2	.18	.03	.07
3	.22	.04	.08
4	.25	.04	.09
5	.27	.05	.10
6	.28	.05	.11
7	.29	.06	.12
8	.30	.06	.13
9	.31	.07	.13
10	.31	.07	.14
11	.31	.07	.15
12	.32	.08	.15
13	.34	.08	.16
14	.35	.08	.16
15	.37	.09	.17
16	.37	.09	.17
17	.38	.09	.18
18	.38	.09	.18
19	.38	.10	.19
20	.38	.10	.19

Differences in natural logarithms, overlapping intervals.

Column 4 of Table 13.2 and Graph A of Figure 13.2 give this information for the random series R2. R2 was formed by cumulating actual flips of a coin and then taking the exponents of the resulting series in an attempt to emulate actual interest rates. The x axis delineates the difference interval which runs from 1 to 88, and the y axis delineates the standard deviation of changes in the logs of the series.

For a random series, we expect the standard deviation to rise with the square root of the difference interval. We can model the relationship with the formula: $s = ct^5$, where s is the standard deviation, c is the standard deviation for a difference interval of 1, and t is the difference interval. If you plot this relationship on a log log figure, you will obtain a straight line with a slope of 1/2. The relationship holds also for the two interest rate series shown in Table 13.2

We expect this kind of relationship for a random series. In Graph A of Figure 13.2, we use a log log scale, which produces a series of points that approximate a straight line with a slope of approximately 0.5. In this figure, a slope of one-half will be formed by a line that starts in the lower-left hand corner and rises so that it leaves the box halfway up the right side of the figure. Since we have found many characteristics of randomness in the interest rate series, we might expect that, when plotted, figures of the standard deviation versus the difference interval will look like Graph A of Figure 13.2.

Graph B of Figure 13.2 shows the standard deviation of changes in the logs of yields versus the difference interval for British consol yields from 1730 to 1961. This graph, like the others, uses overlapping intervals which smooths the data somewhat. The smoothed data shows the direct relationship of the standard deviation and the difference interval based on annual data, in this case covering over two centuries. The slope of the line is approximately 0.5.

Graph C covers the Standard and Poor long corporate yield index from 1900 to 1979, again with monthly data. The slope here is also approximately 0.5. Graph D is for daily data, now for the GNMAY yields from 1979 to 1984 revealing a similar slope. Graph E of Figure 13.2 gives weekly data for 3-month and 6-month U.S. treasury bills with a slope again of approximately 0.5. The final graph, Graph F of Figure 13.2, gives daily data for two U.S. issues, the 8.25 bond of

2/15/1990 and the 8.25 bond of 5/15/2005. Note how close the two lines track and note also the slope of one-half.

In the next chapter we will show graphs for other series that reveal the same relationship between the standard deviation and the difference interval, or the holding period.

For a perfectly random series, the rise in the standard deviation will be continuous over time. The rise will not cease. The five interest rate graphs of Figure 13.2 reveal this to be the case.

When you plot the standard deviation on the y axis and the difference interval on the x axis of a log log figure and you obtain a straight line, you have the following relationship

$$\log \text{(standard deviation)} = a + 0.5 \text{ (log difference interval)}$$

or

$$\log s = a + 0.5 \log t$$

which is the same as

$$s = a\, t^{.5}$$

Since the variance (s^2) is the square of the standard deviation (s), the variance rises with the difference interval, or the holding period.

Conclusion

1. The variance of changes in the logarithms of interest rates rises approximately with the difference interval.
2. The standard deviation of changes in the logarithms of interest rates rises approximately with the square root of the difference interval.
3. The rise in the standard deviation does not appear to level off.

4. The relationship appears to hold for various types of issues, yield series, individual bonds, corporates, and governments.

5. The relationship does not appear to depend on the frequency of measurement; it holds where the minimum interval is as short and as one day and as long as a year.

6. The relationship represents evidence that changes in the logarithms of interest rates are random.

CHAPTER 14

The Standard Deviation of Changes in the Logarithms of Interest Rates Rises with Maturity

In the last chapter, we looked at the relationship between the variability of changes in interest rates and the difference interval and found that the square root rule applied. The variance of interest rates, like the variance of a random walk, was directly related to the difference interval, and the standard deviation of each of these series was directly related to the square root of the difference interval. We expect this result for a random walk from probability theory; we suspect the same result for interest rates evidence that changes in rates are random. The square root rule itself is evidence of the random character of interest rates.

When we turn to the question of the effect of bond maturity on the variability of interest rates, we have only our general knowledge that short rates are generally more volatile than long rates. The first studies we did of this relationship resulted in a fairly systematic relationship between the maturity of the bond and the volatility of rates, after taking into account the effect, described in the last chapter, of the difference interval. We used the standard deviation of changes in the logarithms of yields as the measure of volatility. But later analysis of 1987 data showed that the effect of maturity was not so general as we had thought it to be.

Here we will first look at the effect of maturity on volatility. Figure 14.1 shows the standard deviation of changes in yields against the difference interval for three sets of bonds. Graph A gives selected long bond yields 1900–1965. The top set of dots is the shortest maturity; the bottom set is the longest maturity. For all difference intervals, the degree of volatility is higher for shorter maturities.

Graph B of Figure 14.1 gives the results for four U.S. maturity yield indexes, 3-month, 2-year, 5-year, and 20-year for 1950 to 1986. Again the shortest maturity is the top line, the next shortest the next line, and so on. For all difference intervals, the standard deviation of changes in the logarithms of yields declines with maturity. Graph C of Figure 14.1 gives the standard deviations for commercial paper and long bonds from 1857 to 1936. The standard deviations are highest for the commercial paper for all difference intervals and lowest for the long bonds. There is a definite correspondence between maturity and the standard deviation.

Instead of portraying the data as in Figure 14.1, we can portray it on a three dimensional plot with the standard deviation shown on the z axis, the maturity on the x axis, and the difference interval on the y axis. We show this portrayal for the 1900 to 1965 data and the 1950 to 1986 data in Figure 14.2. Graph A of Figure 14.2 gives the 1900 to 1965 standard deviations for seven maturities and eight difference intervals. The dots rise to the right, reflecting the increasing difference interval. But the dots also rise to the left reflecting the shortening maturity. The shortest maturity is on the far left, the longest on the far right. The set of dots of Graph A of Figure 14.2 form approximately a plane which rises with increasing difference intervals and declines with increasing maturity. The relationship between volatility, maturity, and the difference interval is very systematic.

As you can see in all of these graphs, there is a systematic relationship between the standard deviation of changes in the natural logarithm of yields and maturity. In every case, the shorter the maturity and the higher the volatility; the longer the maturity, the lower the volatility.

Figure 14.1 Standard Deviation of Differences in Logarithms of Yields Versus Difference Interval, Selected Series of Different Maturities

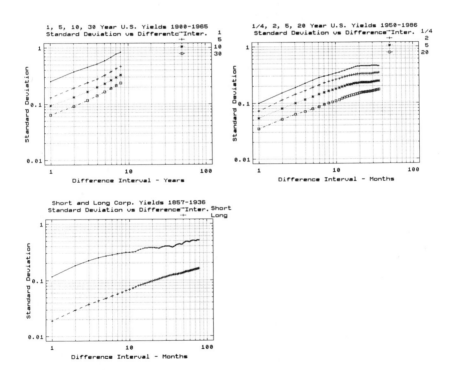

Figure 14.2 Standard Deviation of Differences in Logarithms of Yields Versus Difference Interval and Maturity, U.S. Government Bonds, 1950–1986 and Corporate Bonds, 1900–1965

A

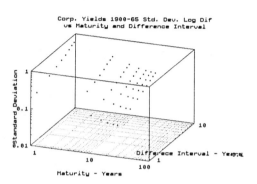

B

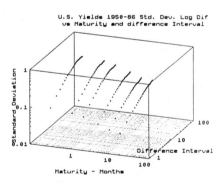

The scale of Graph A is a log log log scale, and since the dots form a plane in that logarithmic scale, the relationship is multiplicative wherein the standard deviation, s, maturity, m, and the difference interval, t, are related as

$$s = ct^a/m^b$$

where a, b, and c are constants.

We would expect a to be approximately 1/2 and from looking at the diagram we would expect b to be less than 1. Graph B of Figure 14.2 portrays the standard deviation of changes in the logs of monthly yields for 1950 to 1986, U.S. bonds for various maturities and difference intervals. You can see here also how the standard deviation rises with the difference interval and falls with maturity. Volatility is highest for very long difference intervals and very short maturities. Volatility is lowest the for short difference intervals and long maturities.

The data used to construct Graph A of Figure 14.1 is given in Table 14.1. The table gives the standard deviations of changes in the natural logarithms of yields for differences of one to eight years for maturities of 1, 5, 10, 15, 20, 25, and 30 years. You can see in Table 14.1 how the standard deviation rises as the difference interval increases and how the standard deviation falls as maturity lengthened. The standard deviations are given as the log difference. For differences of less than 15%, the log difference x100 is approximately the same as the percentage difference.

For a normal distribution, which changes in the natural logarithms of yields approximate, two-thirds of the changes will fall within one standard deviation. From Table 14.1 you can see that for a 1-year bond and a 1-year difference interval, the standard deviation is .25 which represents somewhat more than a 25% rise and somewhat less than a 25% fall from the current level of yields. Over a difference interval of 8 years, the standard deviation rises to .83. To put that in perspective, we have to convert the natural logarithm standard deviation

Table 14.1 Corporate Bond Yields, 1900-1965, Annual Data, Standard Deviation of Differences in Logs of Yields Versus Length of the Difference Interval

Difference Interval Years	Maturity (Years)						
	1	5	10	15	20	25	30
1	.25	.13	.09	.08	.07	.07	.06
2	.38	.19	.13	.11	.10	.09	.09
3	.45	.24	.17	.14	.13	.12	.12
4	.52	.28	.20	.17	.15	.15	.15
5	.59	.32	.23	.19	.18	.17	.17
6	.68	.38	.27	.22	.20	.19	.19
7	.77	.43	.30	.25	.23	.22	.21
8	.83	.47	.33	.27	.25	.24	.23

Difference in natural logarithms of yields, overlapping intervals.

to percent. In logarithms, the yield could rise by .83 or fall by .83. A rise in natural logs of .83 is nearly a 130% rise. A fall in natural logs of .83 is slightly more than a 66% fall. Those are substantial changes. They mean that a 10% yield on 1-year bonds stand a two-thirds chance of rising to 23% or falling to 4.4% in 8 years. Thus, the high standard deviation on 1-year bonds implies very high volatility.

Now look at the standard deviations for the 30-year bond. The standard deviation for a 1-year difference interval is .06, or about 6%. Over a year 30-year yields stand a two-thirds chance of rising or falling about six percent, or between 10.6% and 9.4% if beginning yields are 10%. Over an 8-year difference interval, the standard deviation rises to .23. That means 10% 30-year bond yields might rise to 12.6% after 8 years or fall to 7.9%. Thus, Table 14.1 tells us a lot about how far yields might rise or fall, depending on the maturity and the difference interval.

Table 14.2 gives us the same kind of information for yields of U.S. bonds from 1950 to 1965. Now the data is monthly and the standard deviations are for monthly changes. The maturities are 1/4, 1, 2, 5, 10, and 20 years. The difference intervals run from 1 to 20 months. For the 3-month maturity, the standard deviation over a month is .10, or about 10% meaning there is a two-thirds chance yields could rise from 10% to 11% or fall to 9% in a month. In 12 months, the standard deviation for the 3-month bond is .36 which translates into a two-thirds chance of a rise to 14% or a fall to 7%.

Table 14.2   U.S. Government Yields 1950-1986, Monthly Standard Deviation of Differences in Logs of Yields Versus Length of the Difference Interval

Difference Interval Months	Maturity (Years)					
	.25	1	2	5	10	20
1	.10	.08	.07	.05	.04	.03
2	.15	.13	.11	.08	.06	.05
3	.19	.17	.14	.10	.07	.06
4	.22	.20	.16	.11	.08	.07
5	.25	.22	.18	.13	.09	.07
6	.28	.24	.21	.14	.10	.08
7	.30	.26	.22	.15	.10	.09
8	.31	.28	.24	.16	.11	.09
9	.32	.29	.25	.17	.11	.10
10	.34	.31	.26	.17	.12	.10
11	.35	.32	.27	.18	.12	.11
12	.36	.33	.28	.19	.13	.11
13	.37	.34	.29	.19	.13	.12
14	.39	.35	.29	.20	.14	.12
15	.40	.36	.30	.21	.14	.12
16	.41	.37	.31	.21	.15	.13
17	.42	.38	.31	.21	.15	.13
18	.43	.38	.31	.21	.15	.13
19	.44	.38	.32	.21	.15	.13
20	.44	.39	.32	.22	.15	.14

Difference in natural logarithms, overlapping intervals.

The relationship among the standard deviation, s; the difference interval, t; and the maturity of the bond, m, is very systematic. We can determine how systematic by regressing the standard deviation on maturity and the difference interval, finding the coefficients of the regression equation, and then calculating how well the resulting equation explains the variance of the standard deviations.

When we fit a regression equation to the long bond yields for the period 1900 to 1965, the data in Table 14.1, we obtain an equation of the form:

$$\log (\text{standard deviation}) =$$

$$\log c + a(\log (\text{difference interval}) -$$

$$b(\log(\text{maturity}))$$

When we apply multiple regression to the data we obtain coefficients of $c = -1.46$, $a = 0.61$ and $b = 0.40$. As you can see, we did not obtain the exact square root value. If we had, the coefficient a would be 0.5, but here it was 0.61, somewhat higher than we expected. By taking antilogs of the coefficients we just derived, we obtain the following equation for the long bond data for the years 1900 to 1965:

$$\text{standard deviation} = .23 \, (\text{difference interval})^{.61} / (\text{maturity})^{.40}$$

The coefficients of correlation and determination are both high, 0.99, and significant at the 0.05 level. The estimated standard deviation for a 1-year interval and a 1-year maturity is $s = .23(1)^{.61} / (1)^{.40}$, or 0.23. The standard deviation for a 5-year interval and a 10-year bond is $s = .23(5)^{.61} / (10)^{.40}$, or 0.24.

The fit of the data is very good, indicated by a coefficient of multiple correlation of 0.97 and a coefficient of determination of 0.94. The t-value of each of the coefficients is high, and the F-value of the analysis of variance, 1714.6, is also high. All of these statistics are significant at the 0.05 level.

Thus, we obtain a very good fit of a multiple regression equation to the standard deviation of changes in yields of bonds over the years 1900 to 1965, the Durand bond data.

Next let us look at the monthly U.S. yield data for the years 1950 to 1986. The standard deviations for a portion of that data is given in Table 14.2; the more extensive data is portrayed in Graph B of Figure 14.2. In fitting a multiple regression equation we shall use the same kind of formula we used for the 1900 to 1965 data.

$$\log(\text{standard deviation}) =$$

$$\log c + a \, (\log_e (\text{difference interval})) - b \, (\log_e (\text{maturity}))$$

When we apply multiple regression to the data we obtain coefficients of $c = -2.31$, $a = .40$, and $b = 0.28$. Again we did not obtain quite the expected 0.5 for the a coefficient, but 0.40, a somewhat lower figure. After annualizing the data from the original monthly figures, we can take antilogs and obtain the following equation for the 1950 to 1986 U.S. yield data:

$$\text{standard deviation} = .27 \, (\text{difference interval})^{.40} / (\text{maturity})^{.28}$$

The coefficients of correlation and determination are both high, 0.99, and significant at the 0.05 level. Again we obtained a very good fit to the data, reflecting the systematic effect of the maturity and the difference interval on the standard deviation of changes in the logarithms of yields.

Next, we want to give some examples of how the resulting equations may be used to estimate the volatility of yields, based on a particular difference interval and a particular bond maturity. First, we can calculate the standard deviation for a 2-year holding period, or difference interval, and a 20-year bond. We will use the equation for the 1950 to 1986 period to make the estimate. The standard deviation for a 2-year interval and a 20 year bond is $s=.27(2).40/(20).28$ or 0.16. The antilog of 0.16 is 1.17. If current yields were 8%, to estimate the range of future yields on a 20-year bond 2 years in the future at 1 standard deviation from the mean, you would multiply by 1.17 to get +1 standard deviation and divide by 1.17 to get -1 standard deviation.

Antilog of 0.16 = 1.17
Current yield = 8%
Current yield + 1s = 8% × 1.17 = 9.36%
Current yield - 1s = 8% / 1.17 = 6.84%

You can use these formulas to calculate the standard deviation for any combination of maturities, difference intervals, and yields, subject to the limitations of the original data. Having obtained future ranges of yields, based on current yield and maturity, you could use the standard yield to maturity formula to estimate price ranges for a bond with a specific coupon. Thus, the ability to estimate future yield standard deviations has a variety of uses. The estimates, of course, are approximate and subject to some shifts in the degree of volatility over time, a topic we will consider.

Finally, we want to see how similar, or different, the volatility of similar maturities is in different historical periods and also how similar the volatility is for different kinds of bonds, corporates and governments. We have not yet made these comparisons.

We have already shown that different maturities have different standard deviations, but we have yet to show whether the same maturities have the same standard deviations when they are drawn from quite different periods. Figure 14.3 shows the standard deviations of similar maturities drawn from very different intervals. The first series is the British consol 1730 to 1961; the second the Macaulay long bond, 1857 to 1936; and the third the S&P long corporate, 1900 to 1979. As you can see, the plots of these disparate series are all on the same general line, indicative of the same general level of volatility for various difference intervals.

**Figure 14.3 Standard Deviation of Differences in Logarithms
of Yields Versus Difference Interval, Selected
Long-Term Bonds**

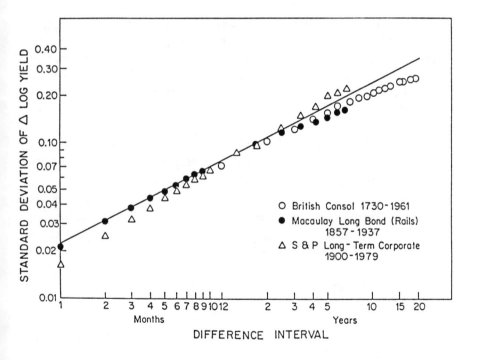

We can also compare similar vehicles in different historical eras. Figures 14.4 and 14.5 show data for three series in
three different periods, 1900 to 1932, 1933 to 1965, and 1950 to
1965. All of the yield indexes are for long-term bonds. You
can see that the similarity among the vehicles is greater than
the similarity among periods which indicates that the historical period is a more important influence on the volatility of
yields than is the type of bond.

Conclusion

By examining the combined effect of maturity and time on the
standard deviation of yields, we are able to derive formulas
that permit us to estimate future volatility. Volatility is higher
over longer forecast periods and higher for shorter maturity
bonds. This relationship is true of nearly all bond series and
historical eras.

1. The standard deviation of changes in the logs of in-
    terest rates rises approximately with the square root
    of the difference interval, or holding period.
2. The standard deviation of changes in the logs of in-
    terest rates declines with the maturity of the bond.
3. For U.S. Government bonds in the period 1950 to
    1986, the equation is:

    $$\text{standard deviation} = .27 \, (\text{difference interval})^{.40} / (\text{maturity})^{.28}$$

4. For U.S. corporate bonds in the period 1900-1965, the
    equation is:

    $$\text{standard deviation} = .23 \, (\text{difference interval})^{.61} / (\text{maturity}).40$$

5. The volatility of different kinds of bonds of the same
    maturity is similar in similar periods.

Figure 14.4 Standard Deviation of Differences in Logarithms of Yields Versus Difference Interval, Selected Long-Term Bonds, 1900–1932

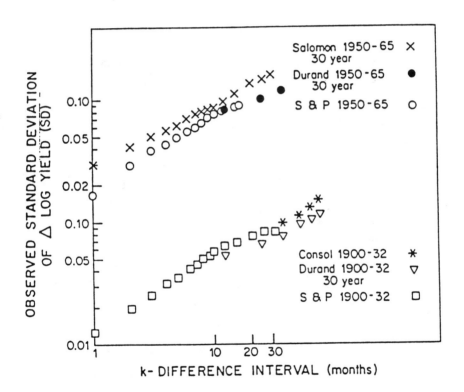

Figure 14.5 Standard Deviation of Differences in Logarithms of Yields Versus Difference Interval, Selected Long-Term Bonds, 1930–1965

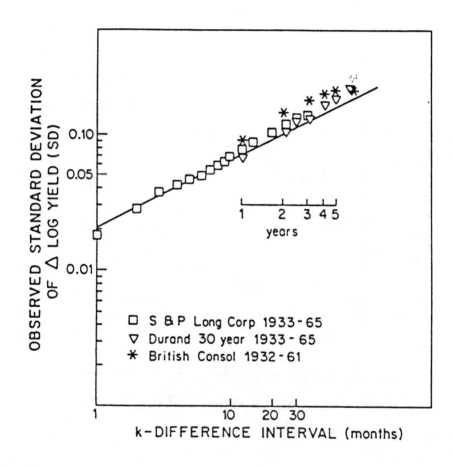

6. The historical era has more influence on volatility of interest rates than does the type bond.

7. The ability to model the volatility of interest rates as a function of the difference interval (holding period) and maturity enables us to estimate the future range and distribution of interest rates and thereby estimate interest rate risk.

8. With estimates of future interest rates for specific bond maturities, we can apply the formula for calculating the price of a bond, given the maturity, coupon and future yield to maturity give us the future market risk of the bond.

CHAPTER 15

The Standard Deviation of Daily Changes in Interest Rates versus Maturity and the Difference Interval, 1987 Data

In the last chapter, we examined the standard deviation of changes in rates for periods of from one week to many years for bond yield indexes. In this chapter, we will examine the volatility of daily changes in the logs of yields of actual bonds as opposed to bond indexes. With the exception of the British consols, all of the results in the preceding chapters were based on bond-yield indexes, not on actual bonds. In addition, most of the results were based on either monthly or annual data, not daily data.

Making this shift to actual bond yields has both advantages and disadvantages. The primary advantage of using the underlying bonds is that we calculate from actual data, actual bond yields as derived from prices recorded by the exchange. We are not using the evidence of synthetic yields, interpolated across a range of bonds of the same maturity or averaged among bonds of the same maturity. We are not dealing with averages, which may be quite different from actual bond yields.

141

The primary disadvantage of using daily data is that we no longer have a time series of constant maturity. The maturities of the yield series decline continuously. For short maturities, the rate of decline is very sharp; a 6-month bill, for example, the ending maturity is 1/180th the value of the beginning maturity. For longer bonds, the proportional decline in maturity is not nearly so great. The second disadvantage of using daily data is that we can no longer look at volatility over a long period, such as the more than 35-year span we had for the Salomon U.S. government yield indexes.

Throughout this chapter, we will use data from approximately 200 U.S. bills and bonds outstanding in 1987, which is the majority of such issues. Some of the tests involve subsets of that number.

Figure 15.1 shows the relationship between the standard deviation of changes in the logs of yields, maturity, and the difference interval for daily yield data for various coupons. The data were broken by coupon to facilitate display.

Upon examining the figures, you can observe a pronounced and systematic rise in the standard deviation with the difference interval. The slope of the line is generally around 0.5, is typical, and as you can see is much closer to the theoretical slope of 0.5 that we find in random series. The slope of the maturity is lower than it was with the Durand and Salomon yield index data, though this may reflect a shift in time period. We don't know. The lower slope suggests that the relationship between maturity and volatility is more variable than suggested by the Salomon and Durand data.

If we fit a regression line to the relationship between the difference interval and the standard deviation, calculate the expected standard deviation based on that regression line, and then compare the expected figure with the observed figure, we can plot the results on an x y figure. In Figure 15.2, we do exactly that for six different coupon bonds using 1987 daily data. For each of the plots, you can see the relationship between predicted and observed standard deviations. Note the high correlation between the predicted and observed standard deviation (with a few outliers). These data, as well as those in

Figure 15.1 Standard Deviation of Differences in Logarithms of Yields Versus Difference Interval and Maturity, Daily Yields, 1987

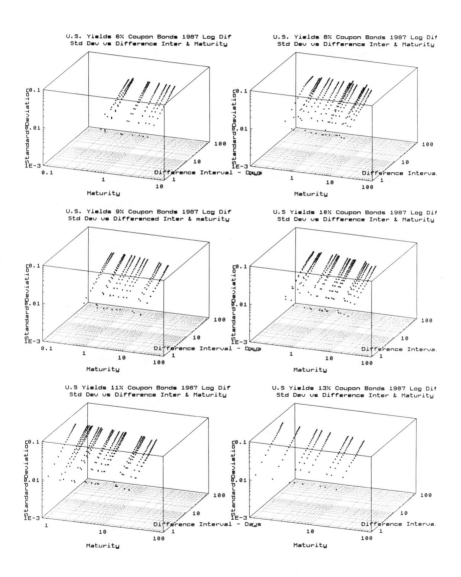

Figure 15.2 Standard Deviation of Differences in Logarithms of Yields Versus Difference Interval, Daily Yields, 1987, Predicted Versus Observed Values

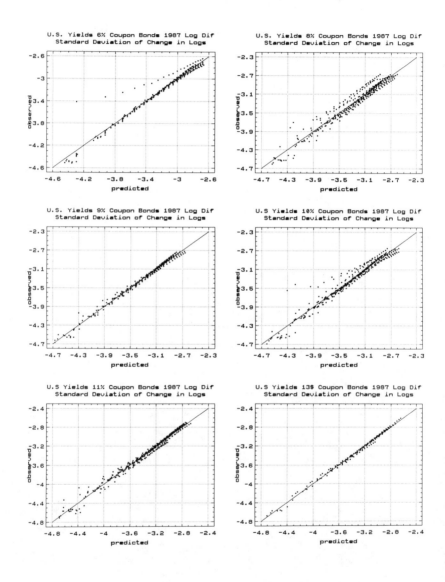

Figure 15.1, exclude four bonds that had unusually high and low standard deviations.

Thus far, we have considered only full-year results. To review half-year results, examine the coefficients and r square for the first and last halves of 1987 for all the bonds in the population, as presented in Table 15.1.

Table 15.1   Standard Deviation Versus Difference Interval and Maturity for the First and Last Halves of 1987, Coefficients of Equation $s = ct^a$

Period	c	a	b	r	F-value
1st half	−.011	.49	.08	.86	2011
2nd half	−.016	.57	.14	.91	3897

There are clear differences between the first and second halves of the year. In the first half, the difference interval has a slope of 0.49, very close to the expected 0.50. In the second half, the slope is much higher, 0.57. The b coefficient was appreciably lower in the first half of the year, 0.08 versus 0.14 in the latter half. The coefficient of correlation, r, is significant at the 0.05 level in both periods, as is the F-value for the analysis of variance (not shown).

Table 15.2 gives some of the same data for different coupons. The purpose of reviewing these data is to evaluate the degree of consistency both between periods and between coupons. As you can see in Table 15.2, all of the coefficients c are in the same range and are higher in the first half, indicating a slight era effect. The a coefficients range from 0.46 to 0.59 against the expected value of 0.50. This parameter is consistently lower in the first half. The b coefficients range from 0.05 to 0.17, a fair range, with much greater proportionally than either the c coefficient or the a coefficient. The coefficients of correlation are all above 0.96. Approximately six bonds have been excluded from the above estimates.

Table 15.2 Standard Deviation Versus Difference Interval and Maturity for First and Last Half of 1987, Coefficients of Equation $s = c\, t/m^b$

Coupon	6%	7%	8%	9%	11%	12%
1st c	.0096	.012	.013	.011	.011	.011
2nd c	.015	.015	.015	.015	.015	.015
1st a	.53	.49	.46	.50	.51	.51
2nd a	.59	.58	.57	.58	.58	.57
1st b	.05	.10	.10	.08	.07	.06
2nd b	.12	.12	.10	.11	.11	.13
1st r	.99	.97	.86	.97	.96	.98
2nd r	.99	.99	.96	.99	.99	.99

When investigating actual daily bond yields, we would expect to get the same results that we got with monthly and annual indexes because the daily yield indexes gave results similar to those for monthly and annual indexes. Namely, the volatility of daily yield indexes rose with the square root of time.

When we actually turn to individual bond data, we find that the standard deviation of daily yields does rise with the square root of time, as it should for a random index. We expected this, but we expected it to be less consistent than it was for indexes. Contrary to our guess, it is more consistent, closer to 0.5, and true of all bonds. You can see this in Figure 15.1. The upward sloping lines of the three-dimensional figures reveal the quite uniform effect of time. This uniformity demonstrates that we did not pick up something artificial in the yield indexes; the rise with time is true and actual.

While the effect of the difference interval is closer than anticipated, the effect of maturity is not. We expected a definite relationship, a coefficient of between 0.3 and 0.4, similar to what we got with the corporate and government data. We do not get that at all. In fact, for 1 day intervals, there isn't much of a relationship. There are outliers, for example, and the short maturities exhibit volatility that is either too close to or too far apart from the longs. Some outliers appear with figures for s and are far off from the others.

This result is perplexing. It suggests that there is a relationship between the standard deviation and maturity that is not the same in all periods or for all bonds. We can say that most of the time—perhaps even nearly all of the time—short maturities were more volatile in yield than long maturities. But how much more volatile seems to have rather wide limits, as suggested by the coefficient that ranged dramatically from 0.05 to as much as 0.6 or 0.7.

In Figure 15.3, we give the relationship between the standard deviation of changes in the natural logarithms of yields and the maturity of the bonds. The graphs vary in the length of the difference interval and the maturity of the bonds included. Graph A gives the relationship for all bonds for a 5-day difference interval. For the very short maturities, the bills, there isn't much relationship. For maturities longer than a year, a relationship begins to emerge, but it is slight.

The length of the difference interval may have something to do with the degree of relationship. To examine this, we calculated standard deviations for difference intervals of 1 day, 2 days, 5 days, 10 days, and 20 days. Graphs B through F gives the same data for bonds with more than 1-year to maturity, but with increasing difference intervals. Graph B is a 1-day interval, Graph C a 2-day interval, Graph D a 5-day interval, Graph E a 10-day interval, and Graph E (now bonds of more than 2-years maturity) a 20-day interval.

If you look carefully at the graphs, you can see that as you go from Graph B, the 1-day difference interval, to Graph F, the 20-day difference interval, the slope rises. The rise in slope is fairly systematic, particularly if you don't count the outliers. Admittedly there are quite a few outliers, but many of these had low coupons in comparison with the other bonds.

Figure 15.3 Standard Deviation of Differences in Logarithms of Yields Versus Maturity, Daily Yields, 1987

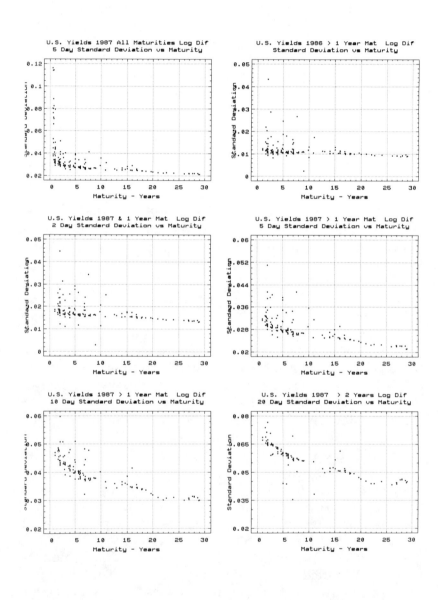

But if you overlook the outliers, the systematic effect of maturity on volatility emerges more and more clearly as the difference interval is increased from 1 to 20 days.

When we look even more carefully at the daily data, we find another phenomena that is also unexpected. As the difference interval is lengthened form 1 day to 20 days, the shorts become progressively more volatile than the longs, as revealed by an arithmetic graph. There is no apparent reason for this evolution toward the anticipated pattern with the lengthening of the difference interval. But shown in the figure, the evolution definitely occurred.

Conclusion

1. For daily data in 1987, the standard deviation of changes in the natural logarithms of yields rises with the difference interval with a slope of 1/2. This is the same result we obtained for monthly and annual yield indexes, but now the slope coefficient much closer to 0.5.

2. The 1987 daily data does not exhibit much general relationship between the standard deviation and maturity. However, as the difference interval is increased from 1 to 20 days, a inverse relationship does begin to emerge more and more clearly as the difference interval is lengthened.

CHAPTER 16

How the Volatility of Changes in the Logarithms of Rates Varies from One Historical Period to Another

We have looked at how the volatility of interest rates rises with the square root of the difference interval and how it declines with maturity. Now we want to determine whether the volatility of changes in interest rates varies from one historical period to another. We want to know whether the volatility of changes in interest rates is stationary and invariant, whether it shifts from one era to the next. We want to know whether there is heterocedasticity in the data. Before examining this topic, we should recall that the volatility of interest rates depends on the level of rates, as shown in Chapter 6. When yield levels are high, interest rates will be much more volatile than when yields are low. Now we want to know how volatility changes from one historical era to another after the effect of the level of interest rates has been removed.

We will homogenize the data, so we have a series that is as nearly the same over time as possible. We can do that by using the logarithms of yields, rather than the yields themselves. By transforming yields to the logarithms of yields, we can determine whether volatility does change from one historical period to another.

151

In the figures that follow, we will compute the standard deviations of annual or monthly changes in the logarithms of yields to maturity, depending on the series. We proceed by computing first differences in the natural logarithms of yields for the series. Then, we calculate the standard deviation of changes in the logarithms of yields for years 1 to 12; next we find the standard deviation for years 2 to 13; then we calculate it for years 3 to 14, and so on to the end of the series. This procedure gives us a running series of standard deviations, each computed from twelve monthly changes. This procedure is used for the Salomon U.S. government yields, 1950 to 1986, and the Macaulay data, 1857 to 1936/1937. Where we have annual data, as we do for the British consol yields, we compute standard deviations of 10 annual changes in the logarithms of yields to obtain a series of standard deviations in similar fashion. For the random number series we treat each item in the series the same way we treated a monthly yield for the monthly interest rate data.

The results of these computations are shown in Figure 16.1. Six series are shown, A through F:

A: A series of standard deviations, one for each successive set of 10 changes in the logarithms British consol annual yields, 1730 to 1961;

B: A series of standard deviations, one for each successive set of 12 changes in the natural logarithms of random numbers from the random number series R2;

C and E: A series of standard deviations, one for each successive set of 12 monthly changes in the natural logarithms of Macaulay commercial paper and long-term yields 1856 to 1936/1937; and

D and F: A series of standard deviations, one for each successive set of 12 monthly changes in the natural logarithms of U.S. government yields for 3-month and 20-year issues, 1950 to 1986.

These standard deviations are presented in Figure 16.1.

Figure 16.1 Annual Standard Deviations of Monthly Differences in the Logarithms of Yields in Different Historical Periods, Various Series

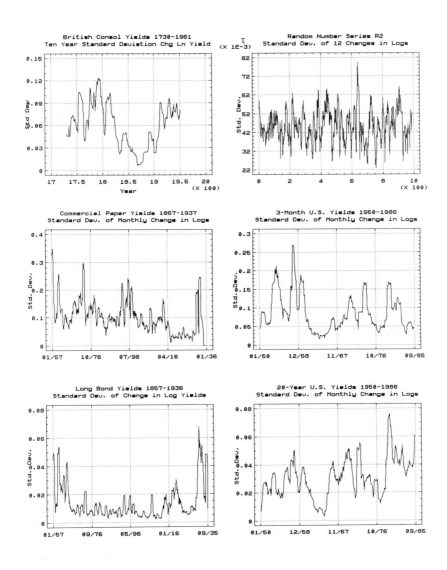

The graphs show the degree to which the standard deviation of changes in the logarithms of yields is the same in all historical periods, or the degree to which the standard deviations are not the same. The random series is given for comparative purposes: to show how the standard deviation of a random series varies and to compare that with the yield series.

As you can see in Figure 16.1, there is considerable variation in the standard deviations of the interest rate series, but not so much variation in the standard deviations of the random series. Quite clearly, the volatility of interest rates, as depicted by their standard deviations, is not the same in all historical periods, but varies from period to period. The standard deviation, and hence the variance (s^2) of the standard deviations, is not invariant, is not stationery. In this respect, the interest rate series appears to differ from the random series. Thus, the underlying interest rate variable, though it appears to be independent and random, does not appear to be an identically distributed variable.

There is a second question we want to examine in Figure 16.1. That question is: are the short and long issues highly volatile in the same periods or in different periods? Is there a coincidence in the time of the relative volatility of the two series. There are three possible answers to this question: (1) the short-bond and long-bond yields are highly volatile in the same periods; (2) the short-bonds are highly volatile when the long-bonds are not highly volatile, and vice versa; or (3), the shorts and longs are sometimes highly volatile in the same periods, sometimes in different periods.

To find an initial answer to this question, we have put the short graphs just above the long graphs of Figure 16.1: Graphs C and E cover the years 1857 to 1936, and Graphs D and F cover the years 1950 to 1986. As you can see, there is not much coincidence between high and low volatilities for short and long yields in the 1857 to 1936 period, but there some coincidence in the 1950 to 1986 period. To help give perspective on this question, we have prepared Figure 16.2 which gives running standard deviations for a longer period, for 60 monthly changes. The use of a longer period smooths out the standard deviations and makes it easier to compare the shorts and longs. If you compare Graph C and Graph E of Figure 16.2, you will see that there still is not much correspondence in the 1857 to 1936 period. But Graphs D and F show that there is some coincidence in the 1950 to 1986 period, though the general outlines of Graphs D and F are similar, the greatest volatility of the short-bonds was in the 1950's whereas the greatest volatility of the long-bonds was in the 1980's. Thus, despite a similar outline of the standard deviations from 1950 to 1986, the shorts and longs achieved their highest volatility in entirely different decades.

In Figure 16.3 we superimpose the long and short standard deviations on the same graph to make comparison easier. Graph A of Figure 16.3 gives the comparison of short-bonds and long-bonds for the 1857 to 1936 period and Graph B gives the comparison of short-bonds and long-bonds for the 1950 to 1986 period. A careful examination of the two graphs shows that there is not a great deal of coincidence.

Another way of looking at the same question is to show the correlation between standard deviations of short-bonds and standard deviations of long-bonds. In Figures 16.4 and 16.5 we show the correlation between the long and short volatility for the 1950 to 1986 and 1857 to 1936 periods, respectively. As you can see, there is very little correlation. Thus, the overall evidence, based on this data, is that there is some coincidence between periods of high and low volatility of shorts and longs, but not very much. The relative volatilities of short and long bonds do not coincide most of the time. This lack of coincidence between volatilities is not at all the result we expected.

Another way, perhaps a more useful way, to examine the stationarity of the volatility of yields is to homogenize the series of standard deviations for each interest rate set and compare those homogenized figures with a comparable number for the set of random numbers. In other words, we will put the variations in volatility on a comparable basis. We can "homogenize" the series by finding the standard deviation of

Figure 16.2 Five-Year Standard Deviations of Monthly Differences in Logarithms of Yields in Different Historical Periods, Various Series

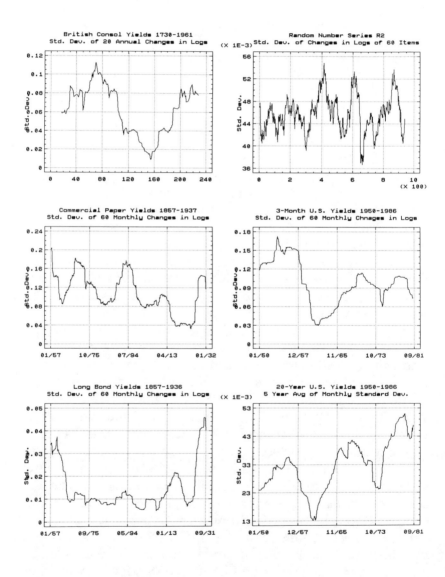

Figure 16.3 Annual Standard Deviations of Monthly Differences in Logarithms of Yields in Different Historical Periods, Short- & Long-Term Bonds

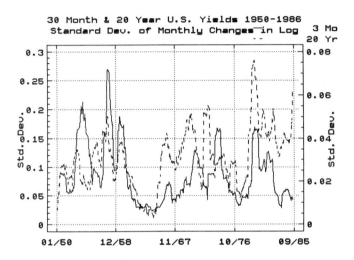

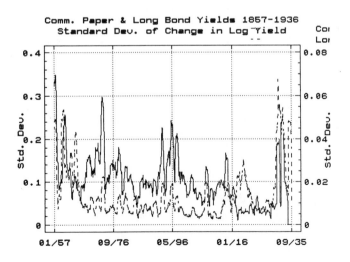

**Figure 16.4 Correlation of 3-Month and 20-Year Bond
Standard Deviations of Changes in the
Logarithms of Yields, 1950–1986**

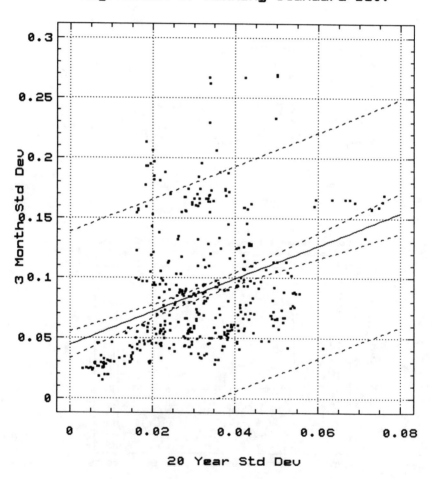

Figure 16.5 Correlation of Commercial Paper and Long-Term Standard Deviations of Changes in the Logarithms of Yields 1857–1936

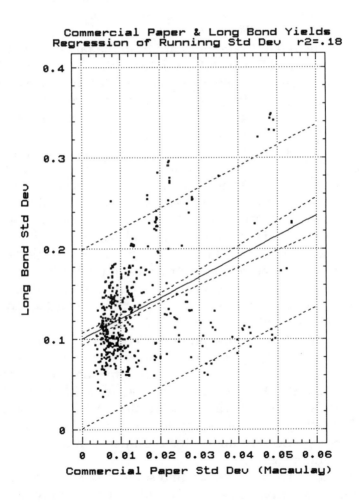

the standard deviations and the mean of the standard deviations. Then, if we divide the standard deviation of the s's by the mean of the s's, we have comparable figures for each series. We make those computations in Table 16.1.

In looking at the table, we want to determine two things: how large is the ratio of s of s to the mean of s; and how do the ratios for the interest rate series compare to the ratio for the random series. The last question tells us, in a way, how different the interest rate series are from the random series.

Column 1 of Table 16.1 gives the mean for each series of standard deviations. Column 2 gives the standard deviation of each series of standard deviations. It is a measure of the variability of the volatility. Column 3 gives the ratio of Column 2 to Column 1. Column 4 gives the ratio of the mean standard deviation plus 1s to the mean minus 1s [(Column 1 + Column 2)/(Column 1 − Column 2)]. The ratio in Column 3 is a homogenized, or standardized, measure of variability of volatility. As you can see, the standard deviation of the s's is always less than the mean of the s's. For the interest rate series, the ratio lies between 0.45 and 0.87. That gives us a rough measure of the stability of the standard deviations over time. In four of the five interest series, the ratio lies between 0.45 and 0.59. If we use 0.5 as a rough indication of the number, that means that two-thirds of the time s will lie between $.5s$ and $1.5s$, or within a factor of 3 (1.5/.5).

The ratio for the random number series is much less; it is .19, or approximately .20. For the random numbers s will lie between $.8s$ and $1.2s$ two-thirds of the time, or within a factor of 1.5 (1.2/.8). On this basis, the variation in interest rate volatility is roughly twice as great as that of random numbers.

The actual ratios are given in Column 4. As you can see, they are significantly higher for the interest rates series than for the random series.

In the above analysis, we find some departures from pure randomness. In particular, we find that the volatility of interest rates changes: first differences in the logarithms of yields are not identically distributed over all historical periods, but exhibit more variability than a purely random series does.

Table 16.1   The Standard Deviation of Series of Standard Deviations of Changes in the Natural Logarithms of Yields Divided by Mean of the Series of Standard Deviations

Series	Average s	Standard Deviation of s	Std. Dev. of s /Avg. S	Range as a Factor
	(1)	(2)	(3)	(4)
Br. consol				
1950 to 1986	.060	.030	.49	3.0
3-month U.S.	.086	.051	.59	3.9
20-year U.S.				
1857 to 1936	.031	.014	.45	2.6
Short	.102	.060	.59	3.9
Long	.014	.012	.87	13.0
Random series	.045	.0085	.19	1.5

We can examine the standard deviations from two other perspectives. We can look at the actual distribution of the standard deviations, and we can look at how the standard deviation of s changes as we increase the number of months used in calculating s in comparison of how it should change theoretically if the series is random.

Taking the distribution first, Figure 16.6 gives the frequency distribution of the random series (Graph B) and the graphs of five interest rate series (Graphs A, C, D, E, and F). The frequency distribution of the random series, Graph B, is symmetric and is the only clearly symmetric histogram in Figure 16.6. Graphs C, D, and E are all skewed to the left, unlike random Graph B. Graph A (British consols) and Graph F (20-year U.S.) are more symmetric, but not greatly so.

Figure 16.6 Histogram of Standard Deviations of Changes in the Logarithms of Yields, Various Series

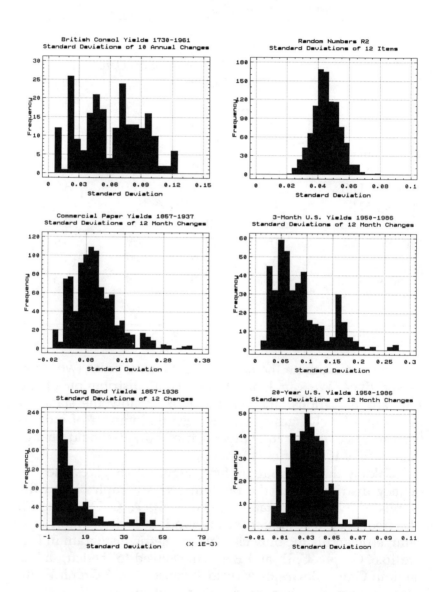

Figure 16.7 gives the cumulative probability distributions of each of the six series. Only the random series, shown in Graph B of Figure 16.7 shows few departures from the straight line of a normal distribution. Graphs A (long-term yields 1730 to 1961) and F (long-term yields 1950 to 1986) are more normal, except in the tails. All of the three remaining graphs (C, D, and E) show significant departures from normality. This evidence reveals overall that the standard deviations of changes in the natural logarithms of yields exhibit clear departures from normality.

Another way of examining the standard deviation is to look at how it declines as we increase the number of logarithmic changes used in its calculation. For example, we looked at running standard deviations of 12 months of changes and at running standard deviations of 60 month changes. We can also examine running standard deviations for other numbers of changes, such as 1, 2, 3, . . ., n monthly changes. Note, we keep the interval of the change the same, the monthly interval, or the annual interval, as the case may be. We want to determine how changing the number of changes, n, alters the variability of s, how increasing n alters $s(s)$.

For a normally distributed population, the theoretical relationship is

$$s_s(n) = s_s / (2n)^{.5}$$

In Figure 16.8 we show this relationship. If the relationship holds in general, then the dots should lie along a straight line. You cannot determine the slope from Figure 16.8, but can tell whether the function fits in general for if it does, the line of dots will be straight. The line is straight only in the case of the random number series in Graph B. It is nearly straight for the perpetuity yields of 1730 to 1961, but not entirely. This evidence corroborates the previous evidence of departures from normality in the standard deviations.

Figure 16.7 Cumulative Probability Plot of Standard Deviations of First Differences in the Logarithms of Yields, Selected Series and Random Numbers

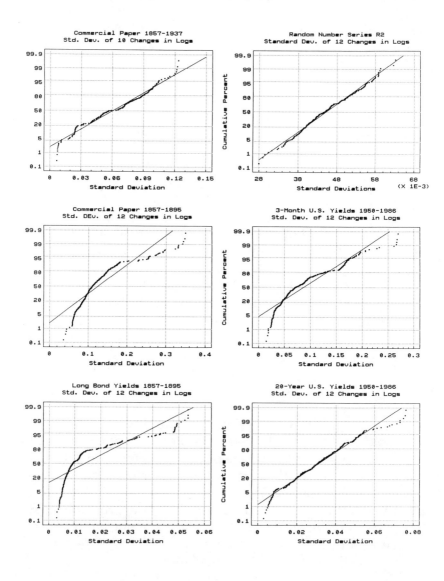

Figure 16.8 Standard Deviations of Changes in the Logarithms of Yields & 1/Square Root of Number of Changes Used in Calculating Standard Deviation

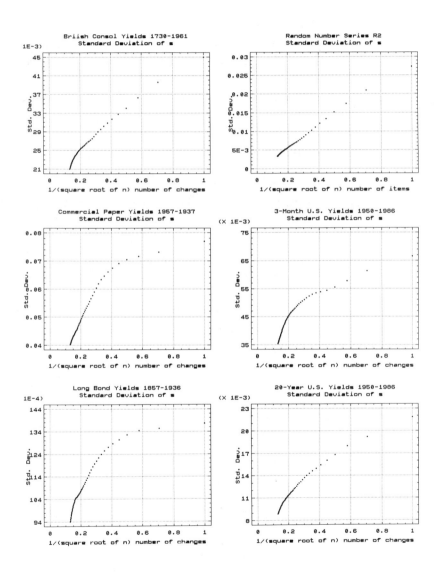

Conclusion

Based on our review of the data, we can make the following observations:

1. The volatility of changes in interest rates, measured by the standard deviation of changes in the logarithms of rates, is not the same in all historical periods but varies from one period to the next.
2. Most of the time, the standard deviation of changes in the logarithms of interest rates, is within a factor of 3.
3. Changes in the volatility of interest rates, changes in the standard deviation, are approximately twice as great as they are for a random series.
4. The distributions of standard deviations of changes in the natural logarithms of yields exhibit departures from normality. The way in which these standard deviations decline as the number of months used to calculate them is not typical of a purely random series.
5. Thus, the overall evidence, based on this data, is that there is some coincidence between periods of high and low volatility of short-bonds and long-bonds, but not very much.

PART V

The Comovement
of Interest Rates

When we looked at dispersion of changes interest rates, we examined the degree to which that dispersion varied by maturity and how it was greater for short maturities. It is well known that yields of all maturities move up and down together. This comovement is one of the most pronounced characteristics of changes in interest rates, and is probably responsible for the smoothing of the yield curve. When the yield curve smooths, its angle, measured by the ratio of short to long yields usually changes, partly because short rates are so much more volatile than long rates. These slight changes in the angle of the yield curve appear to occur at random, and the dispersion of the angle of the yield curve rises with the square root of time in the same way that the dispersion of interest rates rises with the square root of time.

CHAPTER 17

The Comovement of Interest Rates of Different Maturities over Time

In the last chapter, we examined how the volatility of interest rates changes from one historical period to the next and also how the volatility of short-bond yields and long-bond yields is not always high in the same historical periods. Now we wish to look at a related questions. We will look at the comovement of interest rates among maturities. There are three issues involved in the comovement of interest rates. One issue is the degree to which yields of all maturities move up and down together. The second is the degree to which directions of movement persist from one period to the next. The third is whether there is any lead lag relationship. The final issue is how much of volatility may be associated with time and how much with variation among maturities.

Even a cursory glance at a list of yield changes of U.S. government securities will show that there is much comovement in prices between securities on a given day, but that the movement on one day tells little about the movement on the next day. If we took the time to write down yield changes day by day, one column for each day, one row for each maturity, we would see that the rises and falls of yields were, to a remarkable degree, uniform with the yields of all maturities.

We would not see, however, any regularity in the day-to-day shifts; rather, the changes would be nearly random.

From our own observation and experience, we know what is happening to changes in interest rates. We know that the direction and magnitude of change depends on the day or month or year, that the direction of the next change is largely unpredictable, yet that there is much uniformity of movement among maturities. We also know that this comovement may be the underlying cause of the smoothness of the yield curve, the so-called "term structure of interest rates."

We have a general idea of what is happening but don't know the specific details. It may be useful to know, for example, the proportion of the total variance that is attributable to month-to-month changes and how much is attributable to variation among maturities, and which effects are large enough to be significant and which are too small to be due to anything but chance. We can begin to answer these questions by finding out how much covariance there is between yield changes of all maturities in the same period, how often all maturity yields move in the same direction, and how often yields of all maturities move to the same degree. Finally, it may be useful to determine what the degree of correlation is across maturities and whether the mean change and standard deviation of change of different maturities are predictable functions of maturity.

Though these are important issues, they have not been fully treated in the extensive literature on interest rates. Term structure has been examined from the perspective of prevailing yields, not changes in yields. Changes in yields by maturity has been examined with the aim of predicting changes in long rates from prior changes in short rates, and vice versa, by using lead-lag analysis, but without significant success. The analysis of variance (ANOVA) has not been applied to the matrix of yield changes of various maturities, nor have the other issues listed above been addressed, except as noted.

The data used in this study are the monthly Salomon Brothers' constant maturity yield indexes from January 1979 to June 1986. Those are the years for which data is available for eleven different bond maturity indices. From the monthly yields, we compute first differences in the natural logarithms of yields, which, for practical purposes, are the approximate equivalent of percentage changes in yields, within the range -15% to +15%.

The matrix of yield changes resulting from the above operations is an 11-row, 89-column matrix, with one row for each maturity and one column for each 1-month interval. The 11 maturities are 3-month, 6-month, and 1-, 2-, 3-, 4-, 5-, 7-, 10-, 20-, and 30-year, with the 3-month maturity on the top row and the 30-year maturity on the bottom. The first column gives the change in yields between January and February of 1979; the last column gives the change in yields between May and June of 1986. The full matrix gives a broad picture of changes in yields for the various maturities over those 90 months, or 7.5 years. The matrix is given below in Table 17.1.

This table illustrates some very striking features, which you can see by glancing down the columns. Perhaps the most striking is that, for any month, all of the signs of change are the same. When interest rates rise, they rise on all maturities; when interest rates fall, they fall on all maturities. We will look at the uniformity of direction in more detail below, but for now, it is sufficient to see that the general direction of movement is consistent. The second striking feature, which parallels the first, is that the magnitude of change is uniform, more often than not. When rates rise sharply, they rise sharply for all maturities; and when rates fall precipitously, they fall precipitously for all maturities. In the same way, when the movement up is modest for one maturity, it is generally modest for all; when the movement down is modest for one, it is modest for all. There are exceptions to this rule, but it generally holds true. In sum, in any given period, there is striking comovement of rates among all maturities, both in direction and magnitude. This prevailing covariance of interest rate changes between maturities each month provides a sufficient explanation for the smoothness of the yield curve.

Table 17.1 Monthly Changes in the Natural Logarithms of U.S. Government Yields for 11 Maturities 1979-1986

Maturity	1979											1980											
	Feb	Mar	Apr	May	Jun	Jul	Aug	Sep	Oct	Nov	Dec	Jan	Feb	Mar	Apr	May	Jun	Jul	Aug	Sep	Oct	Nov	Dec
3 month	0	2	0	1	0	-7	2	7	3	19	-6	5	0	15	2	-35	-28	2	8	14	15	11	14
6 month	-1	2	0	-1	0	-6	4	6	3	19	-6	3	0	17	5	-36	-28	-1	9	17	12	12	12
1 year	-4	-2	-2	2	-5	-6	4	7	4	18	-7	-2	4	21	3	-34	-24	-4	10	18	10	11	10
2 years	-4	3	-2	2	-4	-6	4	6	4	18	-6	-1	5	22	0	-31	-16	-3	8	16	6	9	8
3 years	-5	0	-1	0	-3	-5	5	5	3	18	-11	0	6	21	-2	-24	-13	-2	8	14	4	8	4
4 years	-5	3	-1	2	-4	-3	2	4	2	19	-9	-1	6	19	-1	-22	-11	-2	7	14	4	8	4
5 years	-4	3	-1	1	-3	-3	3	5	1	16	-6	0	7	20	-2	-21	-10	-2	6	14	2	8	4
7 years	-3	3	-1	2	-3	-3	3	3	2	14	-4	-1	8	15	-3	-16	-7	-2	6	11	3	6	1
10 years	-2	2	0	3	-3	-3	2	3	2	13	-4	0	7	13	-1	-16	-5	-3	6	8	3	5	2
20 years	-1	3	-1	2	-2	-3	1	2	3	13	-4	0	10	10	1	-14	-5	-3	6	6	4	4	0
30 years	-1	3	-1	2	-1	-3	2	1	2	10	-2	0	9	9	1	-12	-5	-4	6	6	4	4	1

Maturity	1981												1982											
	Jan	Feb	Mar	Apr	May	Jun	Jul	Aug	Sep	Oct	Nov	Dec	Jan	Feb	Mar	Apr	May	Jun	Jul	Aug	Sep	Oct	Nov	Dec
3 month	-1	2	-1	-15	18	-1	-3	3	5	-8	-13	-20	5	13	-1	6	-7	-8	11	-27	-16	-11	5	4
6 month	-4	-2	4	-16	18	-3	2	6	7	-7	-15	-17	9	7	2	1	-5	-8	12	-20	-12	-10	-4	2
1 year	-7	0	6	-12	16	-6	3	7	6	-3	-15	-17	9	5	2	0	-4	-6	10	-17	-8	-8	-11	1
2 years	-8	2	6	-7	12	-4	3	7	6	0	-14	-14	7	4	2	1	-4	-3	7	-10	-10	-6	-6	1
3 years	-5	2	7	-4	8	-2	3	8	3	1	-12	-11	6	2	1	1	-3	-2	7	-8	-9	-6	-13	-1
4 years	-5	2	6	-3	9	-6	4	8	4	1	-10	-11	5	5	0	1	-4	-1	6	-7	-6	-10	-12	1
5 years	-4	1	9	-4	8	-5	4	7	5	1	-10	-13	7	1	0	1	-4	0	5	-7	-6	-9	-11	1
7 years	-1	1	7	-2	8	-6	4	7	5	2	-9	-9	5	1	1	2	-4	-1	6	-7	-6	-9	-10	-1
10 years	-2	2	6	-2	8	-6	4	6	4	2	-7	-10	5	2	1	1	-3	-3	4	-5	-7	-7	-9	-3
20 years	-3	4	6	-2	7	-6	4	4	6	3	-6	-8	3	1	-1	1	-2	1	3	-3	-8	-8	-8	2
30 years	-3	2	6	-3	8	-4	2	5	6	3	3	-10	4	2	2	-1	-1	-2	0	-3	-7	-6	-7	0

1983 / 1984

Maturity	Dec	Jan	Feb	Mar	Apr	May	Jun	Jul	Aug	Sep	Oct	Nov	Dec	Jan	Feb	Mar	Apr	May	Jun	Jul	Aug	Sep	Oct	Nov	Dec
3 month	4	-5	3	-3	9	-8	7	1	6	0	-6	-2	4	1	-1	3	5	1	0	2	5	2	-4	-13	-7
6 month	2	-7	3	-4	9	-8	8	2	7	0	-8	-1	3	1	-2	4	5	2	6	-1	2	1	-4	-12	-7
1 year	1	-7	3	-4	8	-7	8	1	9	0	-7	0	2	1	-3	4	5	3	9	1	-4	1	-4	-11	-5
2 years	1	-5	1	-2	5	-6	8	1	7	1	-6	1	0	2	-3	4	5	3	9	2	-5	-1	-4	-9	-5
3 years	-1	-3	1	-4	5	-6	7	2	7	2	-6	2	0	2	-3	4	4	3	8	1	-6	-1	-3	-8	-4
4 years	1	-6	3	-4	4	-5	7	3	8	1	-6	2	0	2	-2	4	4	2	9	2	-7	0	-3	-7	-3
5 years	-1	-3	2	-5	5	-5	6	3	8	0	-5	2	0	1	-2	4	3	3	8	0	-7	0	-2	-8	-2
7 years	1	-5	4	-5	5	-4	7	1	8	1	-5	2	-1	2	-2	4	3	3	9	1	-7	-1	-3	-7	-1
10 years	-3	-4	4	-5	3	-4	6	1	8	1	-5	3	-1	2	-1	4	3	3	8	0	-7	-1	-3	-6	-2
20 years	2	-3	4	-4	2	-3	6	0	7	0	-4	3	-1	2	-2	4	2	3	6	1	-7	-2	-3	-5	0
30 years	0	-3	5	-5	2	-3	6	0	7	0	-4	3	-1	2	-1	4	3	3	7	0	-7	-2	-2	-6	0

1985 / 1986

Maturity	Dec	Jan	Feb	Mar	Apr	May	Jun	Jul	Aug	Sep	Oct	Nov	Dec	Jan	Feb	Mar	Apr	May	Jun
3 month	-7	3	6	-4	-4	-4	-11	-4	6	-1	-1	2	-1	-2	-1	1	-10	-4	4
6 month	-6	0	8	-3	-5	-3	-12	-3	6	-1	-1	1	-1	-2	-1	-1	-12	-2	5
1 year	-6	0	6	-2	-6	-3	-12	-3	5	0	-1	0	-1	-3	0	-2	-10	-3	6
2 years	-5	0	7	-3	-5	-4	-10	-4	4	0	-1	-2	-2	-5	-1	-3	-11	-2	9
3 years	-3	-2	7	-2	-5	-2	-10	-2	4	-2	-1	-3	-3	-6	-1	-4	-10	0	8
4 years	-2	-2	6	-2	-4	-2	-12	-2	6	-2	-1	-3	-4	-6	0	-7	-9	0	10
5 years	-1	-3	7	-2	-4	-1	-11	-1	3	-1	-1	-3	-4	-7	0	-8	-10	0	8
7 years	-1	-3	7	-2	-3	0	-11	0	3	-2	-1	-3	-4	-7	0	-10	-9	0	11
10 years	0	-3	7	-2	-3	0	-10	0	3	-2	0	-3	-4	-7	1	-10	-10	1	9
20 years	0	-3	7	-2	-2	-1	-9	-1	3	-1	1	-3	-4	-6	0	-12	-11	1	11
30 years	0	-3	7	-2	-1	-1	-8	-1	2	-2	0	-3	-5	-6	0	-11	-11	0	6

Table 17.2 Ranked Monthly Changes in the Natural Logarithms of U.S. Government Yields for 11 Maturities 1979-1986

U.S. Treasury Yields—.25, .5, 1, 2, 3, 4, 5, 7, 10, 20, 30, years, 1979-86. Pattern of changes in yields by maturity. Log change ×100—sorted. Each row represents a maturity, short to long. Each column is a month.

First group of columns:

-35	-28	-27	-20	-16	-15	-13	-13	-11	-11	-10	-8	-8	-8	-7	-7	-7	-7	-7	-6	-6
-36	-28	-20	-17	-12	-16	-15	-12	-12	-10	-12	-8	-8	-7	-7	-6	-6	-5	-6	-8	-6
-34	-24	-17	-17	-8	-12	-15	-11	-12	-8	-10	-6	-7	-3	-5	-6	-6	-4	-7	-7	-7
-31	-16	-10	-14	-10	-7	-14	-9	-10	-6	-11	-3	-6	0	-5	-6	-5	-4	-4	-6	-6
-24	-13	-8	-11	-9	-4	-12	-8	-10	-7	-10	-2	-6	1	-4	-5	-3	-3	-3	-6	-11
-22	-11	-7	-11	-6	-3	-10	-7	-12	-10	-9	-1	-5	1	-3	-3	-2	-4	-4	-6	-9
-21	-10	-7	-13	-6	-4	-10	-8	-11	-9	-10	0	-5	1	-2	-4	-1	-1	-1	-5	-6
-16	-7	-6	-9	-6	-2	-9	-7	-11	-10	-9	0	-4	2	-1	-3	0	-3	-4	-5	-4
-16	-5	-5	-10	-7	-2	-7	-6	-10	-7	-10	-1	-3	2	-2	-3	0	-3	-5	-5	-4
-14	-5	-3	-8	-8	-2	-6	-5	-9	-8	-11	1	-3	3	0	-3	0	-2	-5	-4	-4
-12	-5	-3	-10	-7	-3	-6	-6	-8	-6	-11	0	-3	3	0	-3	-1	-2	-6	-4	-2

Next group of columns:

-5	-4	-4	-4	-4	-3	-3	-2	-2	-1	-1	-1	-1	-1	-1	-1	-1	-1	-1	0
-7	-5	-4	-3	-3	-2	-4	-2	-1	-1	-3	-1	-1	0	0	2	4	4	4	-1
-7	-6	-2	-3	-2	-3	-3	-3	0	-6	-6	-1	-1	-2	-2	2	6	6	6	-4
-5	-5	-3	-4	-4	-3	-5	-5	1	-4	-3	-1	-1	2	3	3	4	6	7	-4
-3	-5	-2	-3	-2	-3	-6	-6	2	-2	-3	-3	3	3	1	-1	6	6	6	-5
-6	-4	-2	-2	-2	-3	-4	-7	2	-5	-2	-4	4	4	0	-4	6	9	4	-4
-3	-4	-2	-2	-2	-3	-5	-7	2	-6	-1	-4	4	4	0	0	4	7	0	-3
-5	-3	-3	-2	-2	-3	-5	-7	3	-6	-2	-4	4	-1	-1	-4	4	6	-1	-2
-4	-3	-3	-2	-2	-2	-4	-6	3	-6	-1	-4	4	-1	-1	-4	4	6	-1	-1
-3	-2	-2	-2	-2	-3	-4	-6	3	-4	-2	-5	-5	-1	0	-1	6	6	6	-1
-3	-1	-1	-1	-2	-1	-2	-6	3	-4	-1	-1	-5	0	0	-1	6	6	6	-1

Next group of columns:

0	0	0	0	0	1	1	1	1	1	2	2	2	2	2	2	2	2	3	3
0	0	0	0	6	−1	−1	1	2	2	−2	−1	−1	1	1	2	4	5	0	3
−2	−5	4	0	9	2	−2	1	1	3	0	−4	1	1	0	2	4	3	0	4
−2	−4	5	1	9	2	−3	2	1	3	2	−3	2	−1	−2	3	4	0	0	3
1	−3	6	2	9	0	−4	2	2	3	2	−2	1	−1	−3	0	5	−2	−2	3
−1	−4	6	1	8	2	−7	2	3	2	2	−2	2	0	−3	3	2	−1	−2	2
−1	−3	7	0	9	1	−8	1	3	3	1	−2	0	0	−3	3	2	−2	−3	1
−1	−3	8	1	8	2	−10	2	1	3	1	−2	1	0	−3	3	3	−3	−3	2
0	−3	7	1	8	3	−10	2	1	3	2	−2	0	−1	−3	2	2	−1	−3	2
−1	−2	10	0	6	2	−12	2	0	3	4	−3	1	−2	−3	3	1	1	−3	3
−1	−1	9	0	7	2	−11	2	0	3	2	−4	0	−2	−3	3	2	1	−3	2

Next group of columns:

3	3	3	4	4	4	5	5	5	5	5	5	6	6	6	6	7	7	8	9
3	4	6	2	3	5	−4	2	3	5	7	9	1	6	7	8	6	8	9	9
3	4	7	1	2	6	−11	−4	−2	5	6	9	0	5	9	6	7	8	10	8
1	4	7	1	0	9	−13	−5	−1	5	6	7	0	4	7	7	6	8	8	5
1	4	8	−1	0	8	−12	−6	0	4	3	6	1	4	7	7	5	7	8	5
3	4	8	1	0	10	−11	−7	0	4	4	5	1	6	8	6	4	7	7	4
2	4	7	−1	0	8	−10	−7	−1	3	5	7	1	3	8	7	5	6	6	5
4	4	6	1	−1	11	−9	−7	−1	3	5	5	2	3	8	7	3	7	5	4
4	4	6	−3	−1	9	−8	−7	0	3	4	5	1	3	8	7	3	6	6	3
4	4	4	2	−1	11	−7	−7	0	2	6	3	−1	3	7	7	2	6	6	2
5	4	5	0	−1	6	−7	−7	0	3	6	4	−1	2	7	7	1	6	6	2

Next group of columns:

11	11	13	14	14	15	15	18	19
12	12	7	12	17	12	17	18	19
11	10	5	10	18	10	21	16	18
9	7	4	8	16	6	22	12	18
8	7	2	4	14	4	21	8	18
8	6	2	4	14	4	19	9	19
6	5	1	4	14	2	20	8	16
5	5	1	1	11	3	15	8	14
5	4	2	2	8	3	13	8	13
4	3	1	0	6	4	10	7	13
4	3	2	1	6	4	9	8	10

Table 17.1 also offers clear evidence of the greater movement of the short maturity rates. When rates rise, the short rates rise more; when rates fall, the short rates fall more. Like the opening and closing of a gate, one side of the gate moves much more than the other. Thus, short rates show the greatest change, up and down, most of the time. These three features can be discussed from Table 17.1, but they are shown more clearly if the columns are ranked bymagnitude of change, as in Table 17.2. The first column records the greatest declines, and the last column the greatest rises. The short rates were used as the basis of ranking. Table 17.2 demonstrates both the uniformity of movement in direction and magnitude, the greater movement up and down of the short rates, and the exceptions to these generalizations.

We can summarize the covariance of changes in rates among maturities by looking at the number of months in which rates of all 11 maturities changed in the same direction, the number of months in which 10 of the maturities changed in the same direction, and so on for 9, 8, 7, and 6 maturities. Before looking at the data, we might ask, What would this frequency distribution look like if there were no covariance?

It would look like the left half of a binomial distribution. The probability of 11 changes of the same sign in a random series is very small. The probability of 6 changes of the same sign is very high. So the expected distribution would slope up and to the right. The actual distribution, shown in Table 17.3, slopes down and to the right. As you can see, the skew of the distribution is the reverse of what we would expect for a random series, clearly revealing the high degree of simultaneous comovement, or covariance, of changes in interest among maturities.

This finding should be reflected by the correlation of changes in rates of one maturity versus another. Certainly, we should expect a high degree of correlation between maturities, but we might also expect that the degree of correlation would be highest for similar maturities, and lowest for disparate maturities. The correlation, or covariance, should be high between the 3- and 6-month maturities and the 20- and 30-year

**Table 17.3   Frequency Distribution of the Number of
Changes in Yields in the Same Direction for 11
Maturities, U.S. Government Securities 1979–1986**

Number of like changes	11	10	9	8	7	6
Frequency of like changes	58	10	8	8	5	3
Percentage of like changes	65	11	9	9	6	3
Expected percentage in binomial distribution	.1	1	5	16	32	45

maturities but much lower between the 3-month and 30-year maturities. This decline in comovement should be expected because short rates exhibit much greater volatility than do long rates. Table 17.4 gives the correlation matrix of the correlations between all pairs of maturities. The matrix shows the coefficient of correlation between the 89 months of yield changes of the 3-month and 6-month maturities, the 3-month and 1-year maturities, and so on. The coefficients of correlation are unusually high. For adjacent maturities, the coefficient ranges from 0.97 to 0.98. The coefficient of correlation declines almost consistently as the disparity in maturity rises, reaching 0.66 between the 3- and 30-month maturities. For all pairs of maturities, the coefficient is significantly different than zero at the 5% level. A coefficient of 0.2 would be significant here where the number of monthly changes is 89.

Thus far, we have demonstrated the high degree of comovement of simultaneous changes in rates among maturities, based on our review of the columns of Table 17.1. Now, we want to consider what might be called the *noncovariance* of changes in rates in different, or nonsimultaneous, periods which can be done by reviewing the rows of Table 17.1. As you look across the first row, note that the change in rates in one month tells little about what the change will be in the next month. There is very little comovement from month to

**Table 17.4   Correlation between Maturities for Monthly
Changes in Yields, U.S. Government Securities
1979-1986**

Maturity years	Maturity years									
	.25	.5	1	2	3	4	5	7	10	20
.5	97	91	85	80	78	76	71	70	65	66
1		97	93	89	87	86	80	80	74	76
2			98	95	94	93	88	87	82	83
3				98	97	96	92	91	87	87
4					98	98	95	94	89	89
5						99	98	96	93	92
7							98	97	93	93
10								99	97	95
20									97	97
30										98

month, or a lack of correlation, which implies high variance between months, high variability. How large is the degree of variance? How small is the covariance, or correlation? We can examine these questions in several ways.

By computing the coefficients of autocorrelation with a lag, we can ascertain the presence or absence of correlation across months. Since there are 11 maturities in the sample, we can compute coefficients of autocorrelation over lag 1, 2, and 3 months for each maturity. Table 17.5 gives the results.

There is a clear absence of comovement from month to month. Past and future changes in rates appear to be independent or random, without much significant autocorrelation. This is also shown in Table 17.1, but the coefficients of correlation in Table 17.5 confirm it. Using a two-tail test, none of the coefficients are significant at the 5% level, and based on the square of the coefficients, no more than 5% of the variation in changes in rates in one month is explained by variation in the

Table 17.5 Autocorrelation for 1-, 2-, 3-Month Lags of Changes in Interest Rates, U.S. Government Securities, 1979–1986

Maturity	.25	.5	1	2	3	4	5	7	10	20	30
Coefficient of Correlation											
1-month lag	.23	.21	.22	.24	.22	.20	.21	.19	.19	.21	.22
2-month lag	-.04	-.03	-.07	-.11	-.10	-.08	-.10	-.03	-.04	-.02	-.01
3-month lag	-.16	-.21	-.24	-.19	-.20	-.21	-.18	-.16	-.13	-.19	-.14

proceeding month. Autocorrelation for lags of 4 to 10 years produce the same kind of results.

If the lagged correlation across months for every maturity is low, then time explains most of the variance. That leads to the question of how much of the total variance is the result of the effect of month-to-month changes and how much is the result of differences in maturities. Using the analysis of variance, (ANOVA), we can partition the total variance into that arising from differences in maturity and monthly means and that unexplained by either time or maturity. The results are given in Table 17.6.

Table 17.6 Two-Way Analysis of Variance, Monthly Changes in Yield of 11 U.S. Government Maturities, 1979–1986

Source of Variation	Degrees of Freedom	Sum of Squares	Mean Square	F-Statistic
Maturity effects	10	.002	.0002	.3
Monthly effects	88	4.027	.0458	58.6
Residual effects	880	.687	.0008	
Total	978	4.716		

In the ANOVA procedure, the sum of squares is simply the estimated variance of row (or column) means weighted by (times) the number of observations. The estimate is biased which means that we use the number of rows, rather than the number of rows less 1, in calculating variance. Whether we weight the variance by the number of observations or not has no effect on the F-statistic. What the analysis gives us is an estimate of the relative contributions of the maturities and months (rows and columns) to the total variability of changes in interest rates. Use of squares overstates the contribution in a sense; nonetheless, it is a useful measure for determining the relative importance of the two variables. The F-statistic shows whether the contribution is large enough to occur by chance and thus whether the effect of maturity or time is significant, or real.

Let's look at the data. Most of the variability comes from the effect of time, very little from the effect maturity. The degree of variability arising from differences in maturities is small; it accounts for less than 1% of the total variability. The variability arising from different months, on the other hand, is very large; it accounts for 99% of the total variability. Using the sum of squares as the measure, the variation between maturities is 0.002, the variation between months is 4.027, and the residual is 0.687.

The effect of time is therefore real, and it is not very likely that this effect is due to chance, since the F statistic, 58.6, for the variation in monthly means is significant at the 5% level. The monthly changes in yields account for the predominant share of variation in changes in yields. Time overwhelms all other factors in its effect on changes in interest rates.

This summary of the covariance reflects what we see in the data given in Table 17.1: a great deal of coincidental co-movement among maturities and little noncoincidental co-movement between months. Time brings about the great variability of changes in interest rates; maturity does not.

We have left out one important fact, implicit in Table 17.1 and mentioned above but not looked at systematically. You can see what we have omitted by examining Table 17.7, which shows the standard deviation of returns across the 89 months for each maturity. This table points out the inverse relationship between maturity and the standard deviation of changes in yields; the shorter the maturity, the higher the standard deviation. For 3-month bills, the monthly standard deviation is 0.092, or nearly 1% per month; for 30-year bonds, it is 0.047, or 1/2% per month. Between the shortest and the longest maturity, the standard deviation drops by half. The correlation between the two series, the standard deviation and the maturity, is high, 0.98 (if we use the logs of each). This formal relationship confirms what we saw earlier in the tendency of short yields to fluctuate much more widely than long yields.

Table 17.7   Standard Deviation of Monthly Changes in Interest Rates for Each Maturity, U.S. Government Securities, 1979–1986

Maturity	.25	.50	1	2	3	4	5	7	10	20	30
Standard deviation	.092	.091	.087	.075	.068	.066	.063	.056	.053	.050	.047

Conclusion

1. There is a great deal of comovement in changes in yields among bonds of different maturities. When yields rise, they tend to rise for all maturities, and when yields fall, they tend to fall for all maturities.
2. The comovement is statistically significant.
3. Comovement accounts for the majority of the variability of changes in interest rates. The influence of time on the volatility of interest rates is very large.
4. The influence of maturity on the total variability of changes in interest rates is relatively small.

5. There is very little autocorrelation of changes in yields. In other words, the change in rates in one period has very little to do with changes in other periods.

CHAPTER 18

Changes in Yield by Maturity, U.S. Government Bonds and Notes, 1987

Our examination in earlier chapters of the effect of maturity on changes in yields was restricted to monthly and annual data. Now we wish to examine the question of exactly how are changes in yields related to maturity using daily data. The answer to this question based on daily data may help us understand not only the nature of changes in yields but the underlying fundamentals that create the yield curve and cause it to change.

The data in this chapter are daily yields of U.S. government bonds and notes in 1987. Changes in yield are computed as ending yield divided by beginning yield. While this ratio is not the same as first differences in the logs of yields, it is closely analogous to first differences. In fact, the log of the ratio is the first difference in the logs of yields, so we have a one-to-one correspondence between the ratio and the log difference. In all of the figures in this chapter, the number of years to maturity of the bond has been plotted on the x axis and the yield ratio on the y axis. Years we computed to maturity from mid-1987; which, though this represents an approximation, it treats all bond issues the same.

Figure 18.1 illustrates years to maturity against changes in yield for difference intervals ranging from 1, 5, 50, 100, 150, to 250 days. The change in yield is measured as the ratio of the ending yield to the beginning yield. In graphs A, B, and C, covering 1-, 5-, and 50-day difference intervals, there is no clear relationship. The relationship between change in yield and maturity is nearly random. In graphs D, E, and F, however, there is a clear relationship between change in yield and maturity. As we expand the difference interval, a relationship begins to emerge. It appears that the longer the difference interval, the closer the relationship between change in yield and maturity.

Figure 18.2 shows the same set of bonds, but the beginning date has been moved 100 trading days into 1987, instead of using January 2. The difference intervals now range from 1, 2, 3, 6, 20, to 150 days. Again, there is no relationship between maturity and change in yields for the shorter periods, but we begin to see a relationship for a 6 day change. The relationship is pronounced by 20 days and even more so after 150 days. In fact, after 150 days, we see the typical yield curve. On this second interval, beginning 100 trading days into 1987, the relationship emerges much more quickly than in the first interval, which began January 2.

Examination of even the last graph, F, reveals that the relationship between change in yield and maturity is not perfect. There are some outliers, some maturities whose yields change more or less than others. Overall, however, there is a definite pattern to the relationship between change in yield and maturity, a smoothing of the dots with increases in the length of the interval.

Figure 18.3 shows the relationship between yield and maturity, the ultimate result of changes in yield over a very long period, as well as the original yield of the issues.

Conclusion

We can make several observations about the relationship between change in yield and maturity, based on this daily data for 1987:

Figure 18.1   The Ratio of Ending to Beginning Yields Versus Maturity for Varying Intervals, Daily Yields, 1987

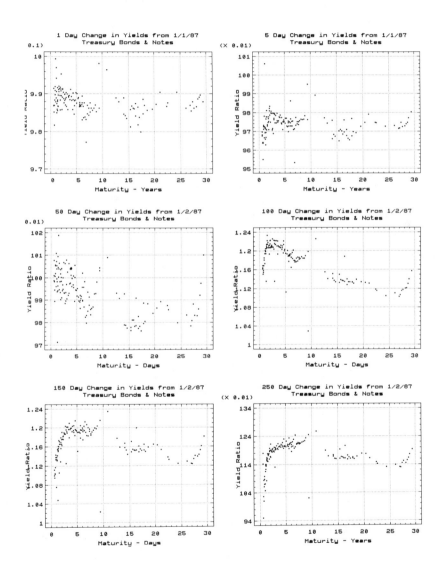

**Figure 18.2 The Ratio of Ending to Beginning Yields Versus
Maturity for Varying Intervals, U.S. Bonds,
Last Half of 1987**

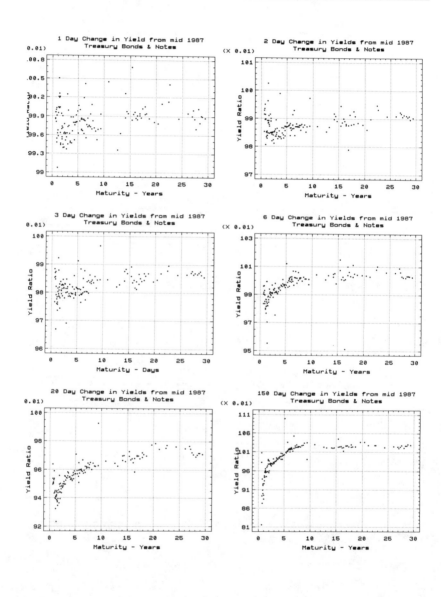

Figure 18.3 The Yield Curve, Daily Yields, 1987

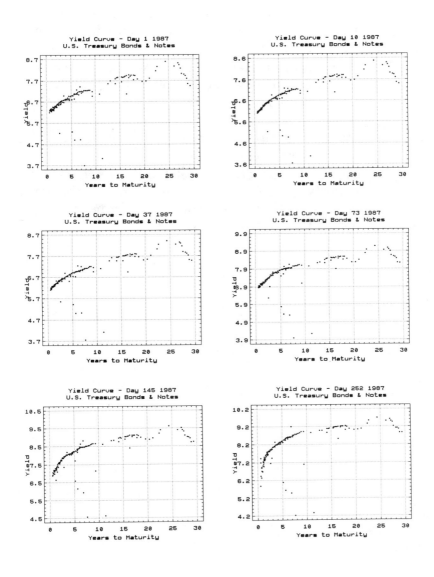

1. Over short difference intervals of a day or a few days, there is no relationship between the degree of change in yields and the maturity of the bond.
2. Over long periods, there is a striking relationship between the maturity of the bond and the degree of change in yields.
3. The time, or difference interval, required to achieve a relationship between degree of change and maturity varies sharply, from 6 days to 100 days, for the above data.
4. The relationship between degree of change in yields and maturity is approximate.
5. The existence of the relationship between the maturity of the bond and the degree of change in yields is sufficient to explain the formation of the yield curve.

CHAPTER 19

Cross-Sectional Dispersion of Daily U.S. Government Yields

Much of the emphasis in prior chapters of this book has been on the time series behavior of individual maturities looked at singly. Equally important is the dispersion of changes in rates across maturities. That is the subject we turn to in this chapter.

Cross-sectional dispersion refers to the dispersion of changes in yields across bonds of different maturities, which is measured as the standard deviation of changes in the logs of yields of those bonds. We want to know how that standard deviation behaves as we increase the difference interval over which the change in yields is measured.

Before looking at the behavior of changes in interest rates across bonds of different maturities, we should consider what kind of behavior to expect. This topic has important implications for the structure of the yield curve. If the structure of the yield curve never changed, then volatility would not rise with increases in the difference interval. In fact, the standard deviation of changes in yields would be close to zero, since yields of all bonds would change in the same direction and by the same amount. But if the structure of the yield curve did change, then the standard deviation would be positive. If the structure changed in some kind of random way, allowing for the tendency of the yield curve to smooth, then the standard deviation would rise with increases in the difference interval over which the change in yields is measured. For a set of random series, the cross-sectional dispersion measured by the standard deviation rises with the square root of the difference interval. For common stock prices, the standard deviation of changes in prices across firms rises approximately with the square root of time and at approximately the same fate as sequential dispersion of individual stock prices.

When the physicist M. F. M. Osborne studied this question for corporate bonds and government bonds, he found that the standard deviation rose for both kinds of issues but reached a maximum for corporate bonds. In other words, he observed a limit to the cross-sectional dispersion of corporate bond yields.

Figure 19.1 gives the cross-sectional standard deviations for two groups of bonds for 1987. The first group contains all U.S. government bonds and notes for which there was a full year of data. The second group is limited to the above issues having a maturity of 10 years or more. Two measures of the standard deviation are plotted, the standard deviation and the semi-intersextile range. For a normal population, the two measures will produce the same figure. In this case, they do not because the population is not quite normal.

Figure 19.1 shows that the standard deviation does rise with the difference interval. We measure changes from the first trading day of 1987 to the last, 250 days later. Both measures—the standard deviation and the semi-intersextile range—rise with increases in the difference interval. The rise is not continuous, but it generally has a slope of 0.5, as you can see by careful inspection of the figure. A slope of 0.5 corresponds to a line beginning at the lower-left corner of each graph and bisecting the vertical axis on the right side.

The cross-sectional standard deviation of changes in logs of yields is considerably smaller than the sequential standard deviation. Compare figures of the two measures. For 1-year bonds, the sequential standard deviation is about 0.01. The

Figure 19.1 Standard Deviation and Semi-intersextile Range Versus Difference Interval, Daily Yields, 1987

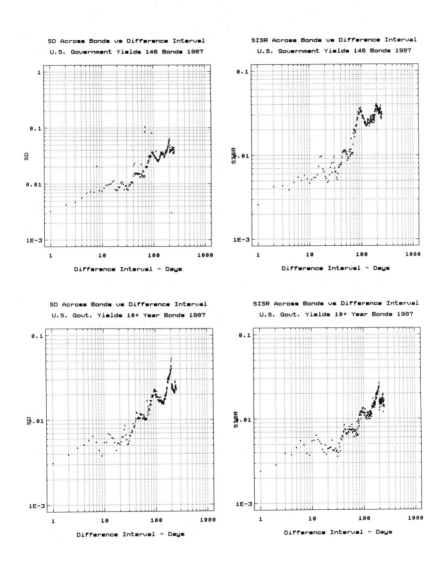

cross-sectional standard deviation given in Figure 19.1 is approximately 0.002, or one-fifth as large. This drop in the standard deviation as we go from sequential to cross-sectional changes in the logs of yields corresponds to our everyday experience that changes in yields over time are much more pronounced than changes in yields between maturities. Yet changes across maturities exist and rise with the square root of time, as we have seen.

What are the implications of these observations? First, the yield curve may be subject to persistent, random changes. The difference in yields between long and short bonds is variable, and the degree of that variability rises with the square root of time. These observations do not necessarily imply that there is no correlation between maturity and degree of change in yield.

Conclusion

Several observations can be made about the cross-sectional standard deviation of changes in the logs in yields:

1. The cross-sectional standard deviation is positive.
2. It rises approximately with the square root of time.
3. It continues to rise for at least a year, based on daily data for 1987.
4. The rise is intermittent, not continuous.
5. The cross-sectional standard deviation for a given difference interval is only about one-fifth as large as the sequential standard deviation for the same difference interval.
6. That it is positive and continuous forms evidence for the randomness of changes in interest rates.

CHAPTER 20

Random Changes
in the Yield Curve

Of major interest to bond traders and fixed income investors is the yield curve. If we plot yields on the vertical axis against maturities on the horizontal axis, we obtain the *yield curve*. Normally, it is a smooth line. Over time, changes in yield move together for bonds of similar maturity. This smoothing tendency is so pronounced that, if you know the yield of one maturity, you can approximate the yields of nearby maturities.

We have looked at the comovement of long and short rates, the tendency of yields of all maturities to move in the same direction. We have also seen that short rates are more volatile, move up and down more, than long rates. When short rates move more than long rates, changes in the yield curve take place. How and why the yield curve line changes is extremely important.

We can investigate changes in the yield curve by computing the ratio of short-bond yields to long-bond yields and then examining that ratio in the same way we examine a time series. If the ratio is less than 1.0, then short yields are lower than long yields and the yield curve has and upward slope which is often referred to as a "normal" slope. If the ratio is greater than 1.0, then short-bond yields are higher than long-bond yields and the slope of the yield curve is down and is said to be "inverted" and by implication not normal. If the

193

ratio is 1.0, then short- and long-bond yields are the same and the yield curve is flat with no slope whatsoever. Thus, the ratio of short-bond yields to long-bond yields determines the slope; it tells us concisely what the slope of the yield curve is.

By examining the ratio as a time series we can determine whether there is anything such as a "normal" relationship; we can determine whether the ratio of short-bond yields to long-bond yields is normally below 1.0 or not. We can also examine the behavior of the ratio to determine how it changes and whether it has the same characteristics that interest rates themselves have.

Before we turn to this question, there are several observations which we can make. We know from Chapter 17 that short-bond and long-bond yields move together in the same direction most of the time. We know that most of the change in yields is a result of the historical period rather than the maturity. We know that short-bond rates tend to be much more volatile than long-bond rates. All of this might lead us to suspect that the ratio of short-bond to long-bond yields and therefore the slope of the yield curve is largely controlled by changes in short-bond rates. The combination of more volatile short rates and high comovement of rates of all maturities should lead us also to suspect that the ratio of short-to-long yields is largely a reflection of changes in short rates. Since the ratio is largely a reflection of changes in short-bond rates, the time series of the ratio should have the same characteristics of randomness that typify short term interest rates.

Moreover, since short and long rates move together, the volatility of the ratio of short-to-long yields will probably be less than the volatility of short-bond yields alone. Since the two series are correlated, not independent, the variance of the difference will not be equal to the sum of the variances. Finally, if the ratio series much like data in a random series, then changes in the yield curve should also be random reflective primarily of the properties of short-term rates. If changes in the short-to-long ratio are also random, then the standard deviation of change in the logarithms of the ratio should obey the square root of time rule; the standard deviation should rise with the square root of the difference interval. If the distribution of first differences in the logarithms of the ratio is approximately normal, then we should also be able to predict the probability of a reversal in the ratio from the present ratio and the standard deviation of changes in the ratio using the same technique we use with interest rates.

For all of these reasons, knowledge of the behavior of the ratio of short-bond yields to long-bond yields, considered as a pure time series, is extremely important. The ratio of short-to-long yields in Figure 20.1 are series that in many respects resemble pure interest rate series. Take Graph A, the ratio of 3-month yields to 1-year yields. In many respects, the graph is similar to a typical interest rate series. The ratio rises and falls seemingly at random with no apparent pattern. Similar characteristics prevail in the other graphs in Figure 20.1. A comparison of Graph C and Graph E which cover different maturities shows the smoothing of changes in the yield curve, reflective of the comovement of rates. The comparison reflects smoothing because the graphs are very similar, meaning that the ratio of 1-year to 10-year rates moved in the same way that the ratio of 3 month rates to 20-year rates, even though the maturities forming the two sets of ratios were distinct.

In Figure 20.1 you can see that the ratio of short-bond yields to long-bond yields, while generally below 1.0, was often above 1.0 suggesting that there is probably no "normal" relationship between short-bond and long-bond yields. The ratio was sometimes above 1.0 and sometimes below 1.0. For the 1857 to 1936 period given in Graph F, the ratio was above 1.0 perhaps half of the time.

When we compute first differences in the logarithms of the ration we have a series of differences fully analogous to first differences in the logarithms of interest rates. The first difference series is given in Figure 20.2 The first difference in the logarithms of the ratio is the first difference in the difference of the logarithms of the two yield series (since log a/b = log a - log b). In Figure 20.2, there appear to be as many increases as decreases in the ratio, and past changes in the ratio give little indication of future changes, either as to direction or magnitude, except in a probability sense. Overall, the graphs given in figure 20.2 are similar to those of random series.

We can answer some of the questions raised above by looking at the distribution of changes in the logarithms of the ratio. Panel C of Figure 20.3 gives the frequency distribution of first differences in the logarithm of the ratio of 3-month yields to 20-year yields from 1950 to 1937. As you can see, the distribution is roughly symmetric and perhaps roughly normal. Graph D shows the cumulative normal probability distribution reveals that there are departures from normality since the dots on a normal curve would lie on a straight line on this graph. The Chi-square test reveals significant departures.

Graph E of this figure shows the autocorrelation function, and there is very little autocorrelation. Graph F gives the relationship between the standard deviation of changes in the logarithms of the ratio and the difference interval. The standard deviation rises not quite with the square root of the difference interval. The slope of the line is 0.36. If we substitute the semi-intersextile range for the standard deviation, we obtain a slope of .5, the square root value.

Figure 20.4 gives the same graphs for the commercial paper/long bond yields from 1856 to 1936. The distribution is roughly symmetric (Graph C) and more normal (Graph D). There is some autocorrelation of first differences, though it is generally low (under $r = .25$). The standard deviation rises with the square root of the difference interval over the first eight difference intervals and thereafter you see some lessening of the slope, as shown in Graph F of Figure 20.4.

We can compare the standard deviation of changes in the logarithms of 3-month and 20-year yields to the standard deviation of changes in the ratio of 3-month to 30-year yields. This comparison, shown in Table 20.1, indicates how much of the volatility in the ratio is attributable to short-term bonds over the period 1950 to 1986.

Figure 20.1 Short-Term/Long-Term Yields, U.S. Government Bonds, 1950–1986

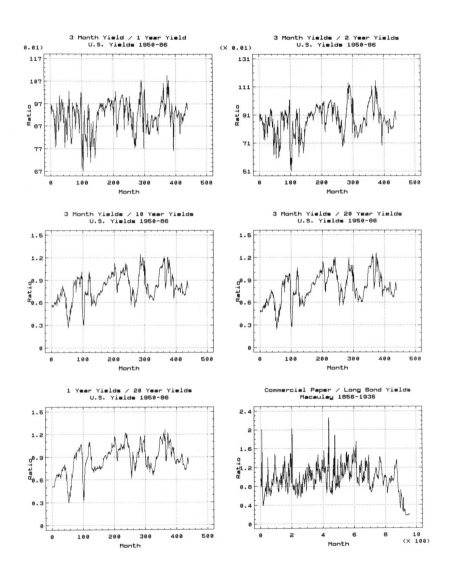

Figure 20.2 First Differences in Logarithms of Short-Term/Long-Term Yields U.S. Government Bonds, 1950–1986

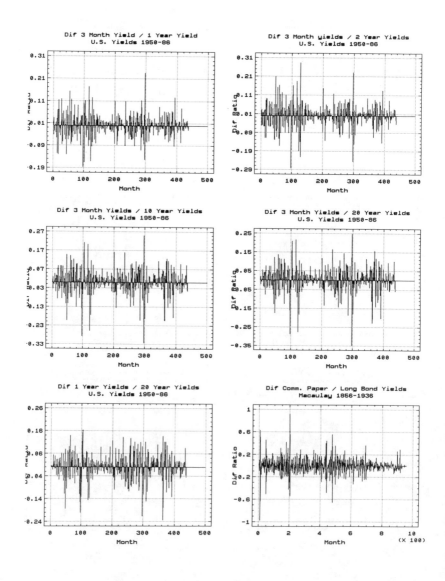

Figure 20.3 Selected Statistics on 3-Month/20-Year U.S. Yields, 1950–1986

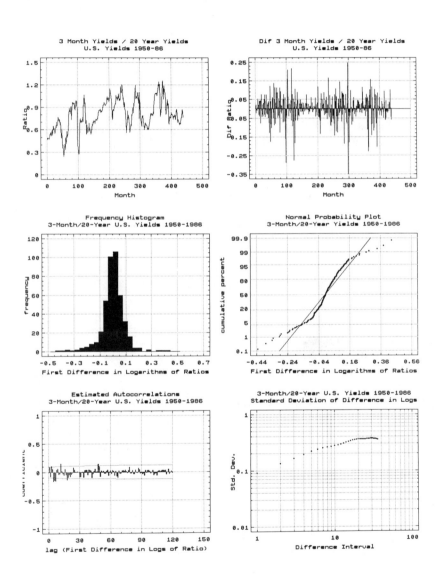

Figure 20.4 Selected Statistics on Commercial Paper/Long-Bond Yields 1857–1936

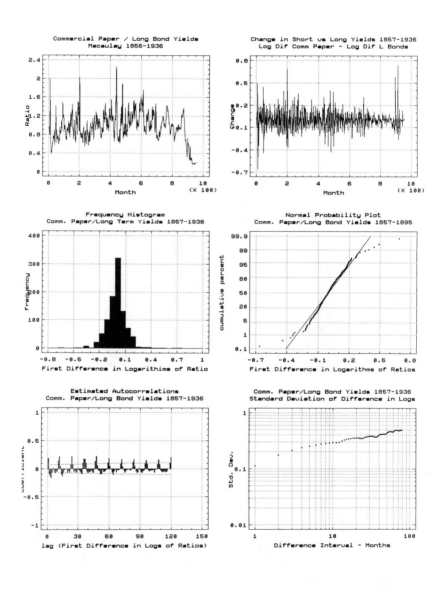

Table 20.1   Standard Deviation of Changes in Logarithms of Yields for 3-Month, 20-Year, and 3-Month/20-Year Maturities

Standard Deviation	3-Month Maturity	20-Year Maturity	3-Month/ 20-Year Maturity
1 month	.10	.03	.09
12 months	.36	.11	.29
24 months	.39	.15	.36

As you can see, the standard deviation of the 3-month/20-year ratio of yields is nearly as high as the standard deviation of the 3-month bond yields and up to three times as high as that of the 20-year bond yields. Consequently, most of the variation of the ratio arises from the short bonds.

If we correlate changes in 3-month yields with changes in 3-month/20-year yields, the coefficient of determination is 0.44. The coefficient of determination of changes in 20 year yields and the same ratio is 0.01. Only the correlation with changes in the short term yield is real. Clearly, it is the short yields that contribute most to the variance in changes in the yield slope.

The slope of the yield curve is the direct result of a random process in the same way that yields themselves are the result of a random process. If this is true, we cannot argue that there is some normal relationship between short and long. What we have is a phenomena that is, indeed, very chaotic and random, not just for all yield series as such but for the relationship between short-bond and long-bond series.

Conclusion

1. Although long and short rates tend to move up and down together, short rates move more.

2. A consequence of the greater comovement of short rates is that when rates rise, the slope of the yield curve rises, and when rates fall, the slope of the yield curve falls.

3. The change in rates, up or down, appears to be a random variable so that changes in the slope of the yield curve must also be a random variable, whether measured by the actual slope of the yield curve or measured by the difference in the natural logarithms of the ratio of short bond yields to long-bond yields.

4. Since most of the changes in the yield curve are caused by the greater movement of short rates, changes in the yield curve are largely a function of changes in short bond rates.

5. We should be able to calculate the probability of a reversal in the slope of the yield curve from the difference between long and short rates and the standard deviation of the difference between changes in long and short rates.

6. The standard deviation of changes in the logarithms of the ratio of short-bond to long-bond rates rises with the difference interval at somewhat less than the square root value, but nonetheless in conformance with a random walk.

CHAPTER 21

Lead Lag Relationships Between Short and Long Bonds

In the chapter on the comovement of interest rates, we found that nearly all of the variability of changes in rates was accounted for by the particular period and very little by the maturity of the bond. The implication of the importance of the period is that most of the movement in yields is comovement, movement in the same period. From this predominance of coincident movement, we can infer that there is not much of a lead or lag component in changes in interest rates. If there were, there would be more simultaneous variation among maturities.

Whether this presumption is correct can be tested by performing cross-correlation between two different maturities for various leads and lags using first differences in yields. We calculate these coefficients for monthly data in Graphs A, B, and C in Figure 21.1 for 1950 to 1986 for 3-month maturities against 1-year, 10-year and 20-year maturities and in Graph D for 1857 to 1895, again with monthly data. We plot weekly changes for 3-month against 6-month U.S. yields from 1977-1984 in Graph E and for a 1-year bond against a 5-year bond using daily changes in 1987 in Graph F. As you can see, there is not much cross-correlation in the 1950 to 1986 data, Graphs A, B, and C. There is a little in the 1857 to 1895 data at 1-

Figure 21.1 Cross-Correlation for Various Leads and Lags for First Differences in the Logarithms of Yields

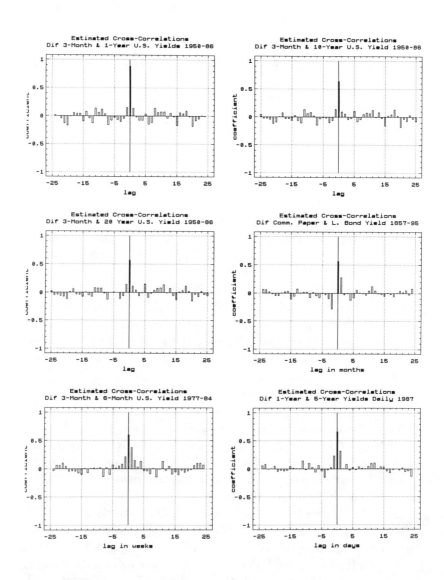

month, but it is not high, .25, and there is little for other leads and lags. For the weekly data in Graph E there is a little cross-correlation at 1-week, roughly .35, but not much otherwise. A coefficient of .35 explains about 12% of the variation (r^2=.12). Roughly the same remarks apply to the daily differences in Graph F where at 1-day lag there is a coefficient of lagged correlation of approximately .3.

Cross-correlation of some of the other series used here produces similar results. This result is contrary to the results obtained by some other authors.

Conclusion

1. There is very little lead or lag cross-correlation between changes in yields of different maturities, based on monthly, weekly, and daily data.

PART VI

The Dispersion of Bond Prices

A lthough the price of a nondefaulting individual bond after the date of issue is constrained to return to par at maturity, the price behavior of the bond in the intervening time exhibits much of the randomness that occurs in interest rates. For a perpetuity, whose price is the inverse of yield, the statistical characteristics are identical. In this section we examine the behavior of daily bond prices of U.S. government securities in 1987 for evidence of randomness.

CHAPTER **22**

Individual Bonds—Prices and Yields

In the previous chapters, we examined primarily yields of monthly yield indexes, as well as some weekly indexes, some annual indexes, and a few daily indexes. But we did not examine bond prices, since those indexes lacked prices. Bond prices are just as important as bond yields, even though they are more difficult to examine over long periods because we lack bond price indexes. We now want to examine the statistical characteristics of bond prices.

Bond prices are, to a great extent, the inverse of bond yields; thus, we should expect bond prices to exhibit the same statistical characteristics as bond yields, at least for the individual bond. When bond yields rise, bond prices fall; when bond yields fall, bond prices rise. At maturity, or the instant before maturity, for a bond sold at par, the bond price and bond yield both return to their original values.

For a perpetuity, like the British consol series, the bond yield is the inverse of the bond price, so the statistical characteristics will be identical. If the current yield is 5% on a $5.00 coupon of a perpetuity, then the price is one-hundred. The formula for a perpetuity is simply:

yield = coupon/price, or
.05 = 5/100

If the yield halves, the price doubles, or 0.025 = 5/200. Conversely, if the yield doubles, the price halves, or 0.10 = 5/50. Thus, the general formula is:

$$y = c\,1/p, \text{ where } c, \text{ the coupon, is a constant.}$$

If we express the relationship in logs, we have $\log y = c - \log p$. Again, it is an inverse relationship.

The change in logs of yield is $\log y_2 - \log y_1$ and the change in logs of price is $c - \log p_2 - (c - \log p_1)$, or $\log p_1 - \log p_2$. Thus, the change in the log of yields of a perpetuity is the negative of the change in the log of price.

For a perpetuity, the yield will be a constant times the reciprocal of the yield. The rate of change in price will be the inverse of the rate of change in price; if one doubles, the other halves. The log of the yield will be the negative of the log of the price (times a constant). The change in the log of the yield will be the negative of the change in the log of the price. To obtain changes in the logs of price of a perpetuity, we simply multiply the change in the log of yield by -1.

We can illustrate these conclusion with an example, using logarithms to the base 10 for ease of computation. Assuming a coupon of $1.00 we have the following:

Table 22.1   Illustration of Changes in Yields and Prices

	Yield		Price	
	Initial	Final	Initial	Final
Original	.1	.01	10	100
Change		1/10		10x
Log	-1	-2	1	2
Change		-1		1

The significance of Table 22.1 is that changes in the logs of yields of a perpetuity will have statistical characteristics that are simply the mirror images of changes in the logs of prices. And for some characteristics, such as the standard deviation of changes, the statistical parameters will be identical.

We would expect that, for very long bonds, the statistical characteristics would resemble those of a perpetuity, since the price itself has little impact as an income component on yield. This importance of price as an income part of yield will be more true when yields are high, because when the maturity is a long time off, the instrument is much more like a perpetuity.

The opposite of the perpetuity, an instrument which has a coupon but no maturity price, is the bill, which has a maturity price but no coupon. U.S. government bills have a 1-year maturity or less. Let's examine the characteristics of a 1-year bill as the price changes. We will take the case where the price drops from $90.00 to $80.00 on a bill that pays $100.00 one year later. Using annual compounding, the yield on the bill is:

$1 + \text{yield} = 100/\text{current price}$, or

$1 + y = 100/p$

Taking the two prices of $90.00 and $80.00 we have:

$1 + y = 100/90 = 1.11$ for a yield of 11%.

$1 + y = 100/80 = 1.25$ for a yield of 25%.

As long as we express the yield in terms of $1 + y$ instead of y, the initial and final prices and yields are inverses of one another. In other words, the inverse of 80 over 90 is 1.11 over 1.25. But when we talk about the actual yield y, this is no longer true. Consequently, for bills, a given price change will always produce a greater yield change when measured in percentages or in logs. A drop in price from $90 to $80 is less proportionately than a rise in yield from 11% to 25%.

What can we conclude from these examples? First, price changes will be in the opposite direction of yield changes. The graphs will be reciprocal. Second, for long bonds, the degree of price change (as, say, measured in logs) will be close to the degree of yield change but in opposite directions. For perpetuities, the statistical characteristics will mirror one another with such measures as the standard deviation being identical. For short-term bonds, log changes in yield will be greater than log changes in price.

Note carefully how we have stated these characteristics. Usually, it is stated that, for a given yield change, long bonds change more in price. We have said, for a given price change, short bonds change more proportionately (i.e., in logs) in yield, but very long bonds change the same in price and yield. The reason we have made this distinction is that we are interested in the relationships between changes in prices and changes in yields. Thus, we have not said in this chapter whether long bonds or short bonds change more in yield. That is what we turn to next in our examination of individual bond data.

Figure 22.1 gives daily yields for six individual U.S. government bonds in 1987. The bonds range from less than 1 year maturity to nearly 30 years in maturity. For all series, there is a generally downward movement in prices until day 200, when prices rise sharply. The rise in prices is much greater for the longer bonds.

Figure 22.2 gives daily yields for the same bonds for the same period. The yield graphs are nearly the reverse of the price graphs, particularly for the longer bonds. For the shortest bond, the bond due on 1/31/88, the price and yield graphs are less reciprocal of each other. For this bond, the yield graph is more like the other yield graphs while the price graph is less similar to the other price graphs. We can make several observations about the price and yield figures. The yield graphs of the six maturities resemble each other and are approximate reciprocals of the price graphs. The price graphs also resemble each other. On both counts, this is somewhat less true for the shortest bond. The similarity and reciprocality appear both in general trends, if we may call them such, and in day-to-day movements. The range of price changes is much greater for the long bonds than for the short bonds: nearly 30 points for the longest bond, less than 3 points for the shortest. But the range of yield changes is about the same for all maturities. In these comparisons, we use the left-hand scale of the six graphs.

Figure 22.3 gives the daily changes in prices of the six bonds. There is a great deal of similarity among the five longer bonds, less with the shortest bond. While the general pattern is similar, the degree of change is greater for the longer bonds. The changes appear to be random, just as we saw in looking at changes in yield indexes.

Figure 22.4 gives changes in yields for the same six bonds. The pattern is roughly the reverse of the price changes, equally random, similar among all six maturities, but particularly among the five longest maturities. Unlike the price changes, the degree of yield change is about the same for all maturities. You have to look carefully at the scales of Figure 22.4 to see this.

Conclusion

1. Based on the data for 1987 U.S. government bonds, we can conclude that the price volatility of longer bonds exceeds that of shorter bonds.

2. The yield volatility is the same for short and long issues for this set of bonds and this period, 1987.

Figure 22.1 Daily Prices, Selected U.S. Bonds, 1987

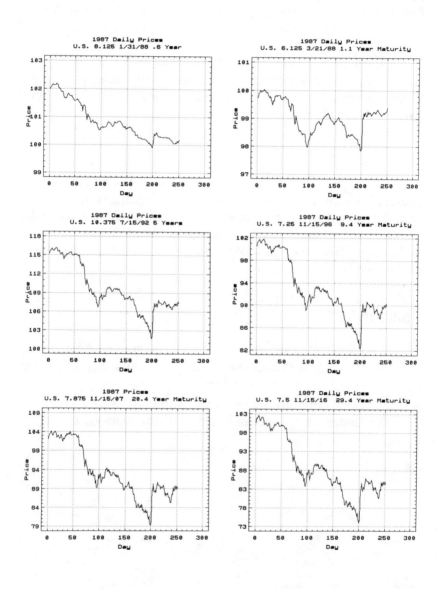

Figure 22.2 Daily Yields, Selected U.S. Bonds, 1987

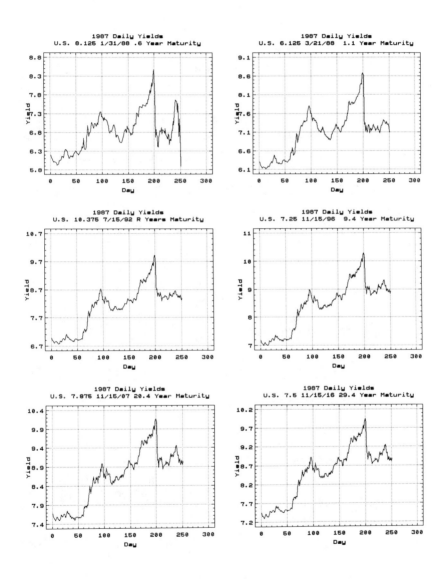

**Figure 22.3 Daily Changes in Prices,
Selected U.S. Bonds, 1987**

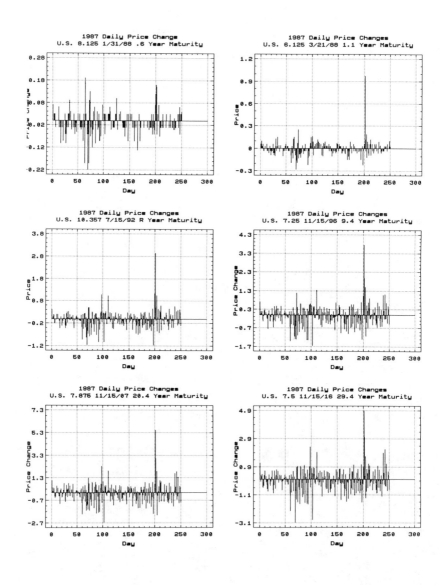

**Figure 22.4 Daily Changes in Yields,
Selected U.S. Bonds, 1987**

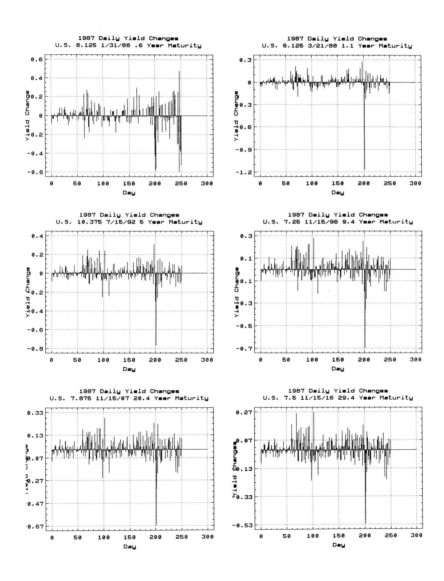

CHAPTER 23

The Dispersion of Individual Bond Prices and Yields

In Chapter 14 we looked at graphs of changes in prices and yields of individual bonds and found price volatility to be much greater for long-bonds than for short-bonds. But we found yield volatility to be similar for all maturities. Now we want to look at how the standard deviation rises with the difference interval for changes in prices and compare that with how the standard deviation rises for changes in yields.

We measure dispersion of changes in individual bond prices as the standard deviation of first differences in the natural logarithms of prices for varying difference intervals using overlapping intervals. This is the same procedure we used in measuring the dispersion of changes in yields.

Figure 23.1 shows the standard deviation of changes in the logs of daily prices in 1987 of four bonds for difference intervals of 1 to 20 days. The bonds are 10%, 5/15/88; 7.25%, 7/15/92; 14.25%, 2/15/02; and 7.625%, 1/15/16. Thus, the bonds range in maturity from less than 1 year to nearly 30 years.

The major features of Figure 23.1 parallel what we found in our previous examination of yields. First of all, the standard deviation rises with the difference interval, and second, the rate of rise is approximately one-half, or a slope of 0.5. (You can see this by mentally drawing a line from

Figure 23.1 Standard Deviation of Differences in Logarithms of Prices Versus Difference Interval, Daily Prices 1987

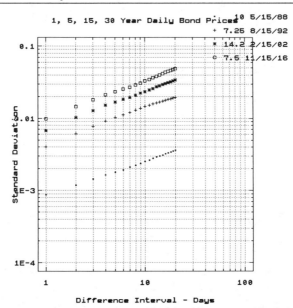

the lower lefthand corner up to the right to bisect the right vertical.) Both of these features are characteristic of a random process. In addition, the lines differ for the four maturities, but now the longest maturity has the highest standard deviation. This is contrary to the case with yields, where the shortest maturity had the highest standard deviation. Figure 23.1 here.

Figure 23.2 is basically the same figure but this time plots the standard deviation of changes in the natural logarithms of daily yields over the same 1987 period. Several features remain the same: (1) The standard deviations rise with the difference interval; (2) The rate of rise is one-half, characteristic of a random process; (3) The maturities have different standard deviations, but now the shortest maturity has the highest standard deviation, the longest maturity the lowest, the reverse of the case with prices.

If you examine the standard deviations of the longest bond for yield in Figure 23.2 and for price in Figure 23.1, you will see that they are very nearly the same. This is precisely what we suggested in Chapter 22. Since the changes in the logs of price and yield for a perpetuity are, by definition, identical, the changes in price and yield of a long bond will be very close. Since that is so, the standard deviations of changes in the logs of price and yield of the same bond over the same period will be very nearly the same. A comparison of Figures 23.1 and 23.2 shows this to be the case: The standard deviations of changes in the logs of price and yield of the long bond are very close to each other.

Figure 23.2 Standard Deviation of Differences in Logarithms of Yields Versus Difference Interval, Daily Yields, 1987

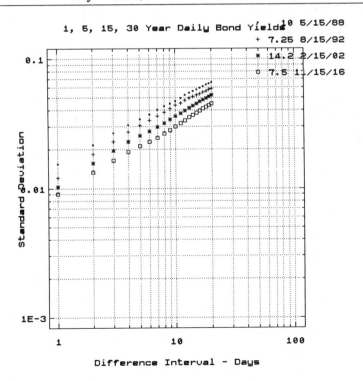

In Figure 23.1, we see that the shorter bonds all exhibited lower standard deviations of price change; the shorter the bond, the less the standard deviation of price changes. This supports common observation. Since, as shown in Chapter 22, a given price change creates a much greater yield change on a short bond than on a long bond (even though the short bonds recorded lower standard deviations of price change), they could, nonetheless, record higher standard deviations of yield change, as shown in Figure 23.2. The higher volatility of short-bond yields, though less pronounced here, accords with the experience of the Salomon, Macaulay, Durand, and British consol data described earlier.

In Figure 23.3, we compare the standard deviations of changes in logs of yields. The graphs are arranged with the shortest bond in the upper left (A) and the longest bond in the lower right (F) of the figure. Observe that the standard deviation of changes in logs of yields is most distant from the corresponding standard deviation of prices for the shortest bond. For the longest bond, standard deviations of price and yield changes are very close. In every case, the standard deviation of yields is higher than the standard of prices, as mathematically must be the case (see Chapter 22). Also, in all graphs, the slope of the standard deviation of prices is the same as the slope of the standard deviation of yields, approximately 0.5.

It's important that we look at the full sample. Figure 23.4 gives the 1-day standard deviation of changes in the logs of prices and yields for all bonds for which there were full data available in 1987 (146 U.S. bonds).

Conclusion

1. The standard deviation of changes in prices is a rising function of maturity—the longer the maturity, the higher the value of s.

2. The standard deviation of changes in the logs of yields is a very slightly falling function of maturity—the lower the maturity, the higher s.

Figure 23.3 Standard Deviation of Differences in Logarithms of Prices and Yields Versus Difference Interval, Daily Data, 1987

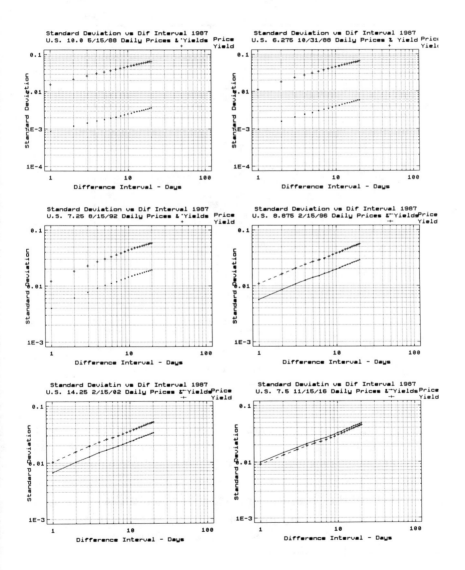

**Figure 23.4 Standard Deviation of Differences in Logarithms
of Prices and Yields Versus Maturity,
Daily Data, 1987**

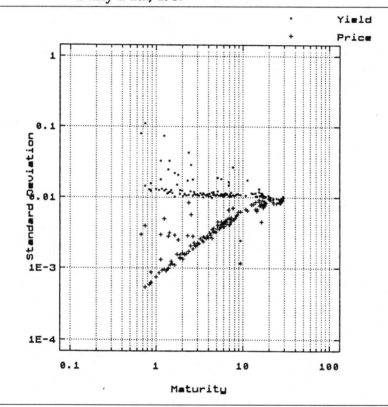

3. The standard deviation of changes in yields is always
    higher than the standard deviation of changes in
    prices, by definition and by observation.
4. The volatility of yield of every maturity is higher
    than the volatility of price of any maturity.
5. There are a number of outliers, or exceptions to the
    general trend. Some of these outliers are bonds with
    very low coupons.

PART VII

Other Evidence
of Randomness

While the earlier sections depended in part on the distribution of yield data, this section uses nonparametric tests of randomness that do not depend on the underlying distribution of the data. The nonparametric tests of randomness in this section include tests of runs, turning points, signs, signed rankings. In addition, we look at autocorrelation, spectral analysis, and short-term time series forecasting methods.

CHAPTER 24

Tests of Randomness— Signs Tests

In previous chapters of this book we looked at several characteristics of interest rates, particularly changes in the logarithms of interest rates. We found changes to be unpredictable from observations, to form a bell-shaped distribution, and to have a standard deviation that rose approximately with the square root of the difference interval. Now we wish to look at other tests of randomness, tests that do not rely on the underlying distribution of changes in interest rates.

Although most tests depend on the underlying nature of the distribution of changes in rates, the *nonparametric* tests are independent of the underlying distribution of the data. This independence is important because the distribution of changes in interest rates is only approximately normal.

Nonparametric tests examine only certain characteristics of the data. By so restricting our examination, we can apply a standard distribution, such as the binomial distribution. In the *signs test* we look only at the number of increases and decreases in a series (i.e., to the sign of change), purposely neglecting the magnitude of change. We ignore all of the information about magnitude and retain only the information about sign of change, positive or negative.

There is a close parallel between the sign of change in a time series and the probability contained in tossing a coin.

When you toss a coin, there are only two possible outcomes: heads or tails, H or T. Likewise, there are only two possibilities in a time series, increase or decrease, + or –.

We know the probability involved of getting any number, or sequence, or set of sequences of heads and tails, such as getting all heads, all tails, one head and the rest tails, or half heads and half tails. The probability of getting any number of heads is equal to the number of ways of tossing that number of heads in n tosses divided by the number of ways of tossing a coin n times. Thus, if you toss a coin two times, the probability of getting two heads is 25%.

By extension, we can calculate the probability of getting any number of heads or tails. The probabilities so calculated form the binomial distribution. As n becomes larger, the binomial distribution approaches the normal distribution, and we can use the normal for the binomial.

We can apply these probabilities to the number and pattern of increases and decreases in interest rates. If the changes are random, with an equal probability of increase and decrease, then we should expect that, in the long run, the number of increases will be half the total number of changes. Although the probability of the number being half is actually very small, the probability of it being close to half is rather large. Correspondingly, the probability of the number being far from one-half is very small.

For example, in the interest rate series, if we have 100 changes and 50 are positive, then we have precisely the number expected if the probability of an increase were one half. That's the number expected from the binomial distribution of coin flips, the number expected from a random series of zero mean. But if the number of increases is 60 and hence the number of decreases is 40, we have a difference of 10 from the expected value.

By using the binomial distribution, we can calculate the probability of getting 60 increases in 100 changes. To find the probability, we compute $z = (60\text{-}50) / (0.5 \times 100^{.5}) = 10/5 = 2$. Using the normal approximation of the binomial, we find the probability of a z value of 2 is less than 5%. If we apply the

5% cutoff for significance, we would say that 60 is too far from 50 and conclude that the series was not random.

Note that, in applying this test, we have not assumed that the distribution of interest rate changes conforms to the normal distribution or to any other distribution, but that the signs of the changes conform to the normal distribution. The assumption about the signs is far less restrictive than the assumption about magnitudes.

Before we look at the data, we should make one matter clear. If we test changes in interest rates on this or any other basis and we use different maturities for the same period, we are double-counting, since changes in one maturity reflect changes in all other maturities (particularly for maturities close together). That means, in effect, that we can use only one maturity if we want to examine say the 1950 to 1986 data. We're going to use more than one maturity for each period, but the caution should be kept in mind.

Let's look at the Salomon U.S. series first for the period 1950 to 1986. During this period, there were 437 changes with a mean number of increases of 218.5. The actual data for the six maturities that cover the entire period are presented in Table 24.1. As you can see, the actual number of increases exceeded the expected number by 20 or more, a little more than 10%, in all years and by a significant amount in three of the five years.

Next, let's look at the Durand data in Table 24.2. These are annual data covering the years 1900 to 1961; there is some overlap but not a lot. The total number of changes in this earlier period is 65, and the expected number of increases is 32.5. Now, in every case, the number of increases suggests a random series, for the actual number of increases is close to the expected number, differing by at most 2, somewhat less than 10%. Here, we have evidence of randomness, though, in fact, the percentage difference between expected and actual is a little under 10% versus a little over 10% in the case of the Salomon data. The reason for the sharp distinction in probabilities is that we have a smaller sample. Also note that, for the Durand data, decreases predominate, whereas for the Salomon data, increases predominate.

**Table 24.1   The Number of Increases in Yields of U.S.
Government Yield Indexes, 1950–1986,
and the Probability of Getting
that Number if the Series is Random**

Maturity	Increases	Probability
3 months	243	.021[*]
1 year	239	.056
2 years	245	.013[*]
5 years	245	.013[*]
10 years	248	.006[*]
20 years	239	.055

[*]Significant at 5% level of significance

**Table 24.2   Number of Increases in Yields of Corporate
Bonds Indexes, 1900–1965, and the Probability
of that Number in a Random Series**

Maturity	Number	Probability
1 year	34	.80
5 years	31	.80
10 years	31	.80
15 years	32	1.00
20 years	32	1.00
25 years	32	1.00
30 years	30	.62

Next, we turn to the Macaulay, S&P, and British data for the last half of the nineteenth century and the first half of the twentieth, the data overlap for 37 years. This is the longest monthly series we have, 960 observations. The results are given in Table 24.3.

As indicated by the asterisks, the actual number of increases is less than the expected by perhaps 15% for both the Macaulay series. Yet it is very close to that expected for the British consol series, the longest set of data we have, over two-and-one-quarter centuries. Similar tests on 3- and 6-month U.S. bill indexes, 1977 to 1986, show that the number of increases is not significantly different from zero at the 5% level, indicating randomness.

Table 24.3 Number of Increases in Yields and Probability of Getting that Number in a Random Series, Macaulay, S&P, and British Consol Data

	Actual	*Expected Probability*	*Number of Increases*
Comm. Paper 1857–1937	430	480	.001*
Long Bonds 1857–1936	406	478	.00*
S&P Long 1900–1979	435	378.5	.005*
British Consol 1730–1961	116	115.5	1.00

*Significantly different from zero at .05 level, indicating nonrandomness.

Conclusion

The following conclusions apply on the assumption that the expected number of changes in the series is zero.

1. In the British consol series, 1730 to 1961, the number of increases does not differ significantly from one

half the total number of changes, suggesting randomness.

2. In the Durand data, 1900 to 1965, the number of increases is close to one half, again suggesting randomness.

3. In the Salomon data 1950 to 1986, there are more increases than expected.

4. In the Macaulay data 1857 to 1936, there are fewer increases than expected.

5. Significant departures constitute variances of 10% to 15% from the expected values.

6. All of this suggests that the signs of changes in yields are more often than not random. However, at times there are somewhat more increases or decreases than we would expect from a perfectly random series.

CHAPTER 25

Runs—More Evidence of Randomness

Having looked at the number of increases in yields as a measure of randomness, we now want to look at another test of randomness, the *runs test*. In Chapter 24 we looked at a single pair of numbers, the number of increases in yields and the number of decreases. If the numbers were close, if the incidence of increases and decreases were about the same, we concluded that the series were random. As a check on the closeness, we looked at the probability of getting that many increases and decreases. For the most part, the signs test suggested randomness.

A moment's thought shows that the number of increases and decreases could be precisely the same yet the series could be completely nonrandom. Consider the situation where all of the increases occurred in the first part of the period and all of the decreases in the second part. In this clearly nonrandom series, the graph of the yields would look like a mountain peak: a continuously rising slope followed by a continuously falling slope. Such a figure is anything but random so that the signs test is not an infallible proof of randomness.

The runs test looks at the number of runs in a series, or the number of times the series moves up and down; this count excludes the length of the run. If the series moves up five times and down six, the series has a total of 11 runs. A rising run is a consistent set of increases in the series, preceded by and followed by a fall. Conversely, a falling run is a set of declines in yields, separated by rises or the end of the series at either end.

The following series illustrates the concept of runs:

$$1\ 2\ 3\ 4\ 3\ 2\ 1\ 2\ 2\ 3\ 4$$

As you can see, the series rises to 4, falls to 1, and then rises again to 4. There are three runs, a rise, a fall, and a rise. In making this test a no change in yield is not counted, so the series of rising yields with a no change in the middle is counted as a single run.

The number of runs is closely related to the number of turning points, since a turning point is defined as a change in direction of the series, a peak or trough in the series, a point at which adjacent points are either above, or below. In the above series, there are two turning points: one at the peak of 4 and another at the trough of 1. Thus, that series has three runs and two turning points. The number of turning points is always one less than the number of runs.

Further examination shows that the number of runs and turning points must lie between certain limits. For a continuously rising series, there is only one run and no turning point. The same is true for a continuously falling series and for a series that is always the same. For a completely fluctuating series, every element will be a run, so the number of runs will equal the number of elements. Thus, the number of runs for a series of n elements lie between 1 and n runs and between 0 and $n - 1$ turning points. The mean number of turning points in a random series is equal to $2/3\ (n - 2)$. Kendall *Time-Series*, page 22.

$$\text{mean} = (2/3)\ (n - 2)$$

The variance of the mean can be found by squaring equation (1) on the right:

$$\text{variance} = (16n - 29)/90$$

Given the number of items in the series and the number of turning points, we can estimate of the mean and variance and then calculate the probability of getting any particular number of turning points in a series. From the variance, we can calculate the standard deviation:

$$s = [(16n - 29)/90]^{0.5}$$

With s, we can calculate $z = x/s$ and, given the normal distribution and a large sample, find the probability of any departure from the expected number of turning points in a random series.

Before we commence with the tests, some preliminary issues must be raised concerning the series to be tested. Should the turning-points test be applied to the yield series itself or to the first differences in the logarithms of yields? Note that the signs test is applied to the original yield series.

It is our hypothesis that the yield series may be considered the exponents of a running sum of a series of log differences in yields and, further, that a log-difference series is random. In this view, the yield series we see is a cumulative sum of another set of numbers. If yields are a cumulative sum, each yield is related to the prior yield and to all yields before. If this is true, then certainly, the successive yields are not independent, and if they're not independent, they certainly can't be random.

Now, let's look at a set of random numbers and the exponents of their cumulative sum, or their running sum. The first series was generated by the APL random-number generator; results for the original random numbers and for their running sum, or running cumulation, are shown in Table 25.1. The second series, shown in Table 25.2, was generated by a series of 10,000 random numbers contained in the IBM Basic program. These numbers were cumulated, and then a set of 1000 numbers was taken by selecting the original series at fixed intervals of 10. Then the 1,000 were then cumulated and their exponents were found. The exponent series represent the yields. The first difference in the logs of the exponents represent the random series.

Table 25.1   Tests of Randomness 29 APL Random Numbers

	Random Series	Running Sum of Random Series
Turning Points		
Actual	18	14
Expected	18.7	18.7
Probability	.77	.037*
Runs		
Actual	19	15
Expected	19.7	19.7
Probability	.77	.037*
Signs		
Negative	14	14
Positive	15	15
Probability	1.0	1.0

*Significant at 5% level of significance

Table 25.2   Tests of Randomness 10,000 Basic Random Numbers

	Random Series	Exponents of Running Sum of Random Series
Turning Points		
Actual	664	492
Expected	664.7	665.3
Probability	.96	.000*
Runs		
Actual	665	493
Expected	665.7	666.3
Probability	.96	.000*
Signs		
Negative	468	458
Positive	526	466
Probability	.071	.82

*Significant at 5% level of significance.

We would expect to find randomness in the original random series, but not in the exponents of the cumulated random series. Let's look at the data. The asterisked figures (*) tell us to reject the hypotheses of randomness at the 0.05 level. Those series are different from a random series.

The key number to look at in examining these tables is the probability. If the probability is very small, 0.05 or less, we reject the hypothesis that the series is random. The asterisked items indicate nonrandomness. As you can see, none of the original random series is asterisked; all meet the tests of randomness. The situation is quite different, however, for the exponential series. There are too few turning points and too few runs to accept randomness in the exponential series, even though the signs tests shows both series to be random.

Thus, even though changes in the logs of yields may be random on the basis of turning-points or runs tests, the yields themselves may not be random. The two series may be expected to reveal quite different characteristics on the basis of these tests. With that in mind, let's now look at the results of the tests on interest rates.

We can examine first differences in the natural logarithms of interest rates to determine whether or not they depart significantly from randomness. Our hypothesis is that they are random. We can use the turning-points test to determine whether the expected and actual numbers of turning points in each series are sufficiently close to accept or reject randomness. We use the 0.05 level of significance with a two-tailed test. If the probability of actual and expected runs is 0.05 or less, we reject the hypothesis of randomness. Otherwise, we accept that the series are random. The results are shown in Table 25.3.

For most of the series, the number of turning points is sufficiently close to the expected number to accept randomness. The acceptance of randomness applies to all the Salomon series, to the Durand series, and to the very long consol series covering nearly two-and-one-half centuries. Three of the series—the two Macaulay series and the S&P long-bond series—have two few turning points. Thus, based on turning

**Table 25.3   Turning Points of First Differences in Logs
of Yields**

Maturity	Actual Turns	Expected Turns	Probability of Difference
U.S. Government Yields, 1950–1986			
3 month	286	290	.65
1 year	276	290	.11
2 years	292	290	.25
5 years	290	290	1.00
10 years	290	290	1.00
20 years	286	290	.65
Durand Corporate 1900–1965			
1 year	44	42	.55
5 years	42	42	1.00
10 years	42	42	1.00
15 years	42	42	1.00
20 years	40	42	.55
25 years	40	42	.55
Macaulay 1857–1936/7			
Commercial Paper	536	639	.00*
Long Corporate	522	636	.00*
British Consol 1730–1961	144	152	.18
S&P Long 1900–79	566	637	.00*

*Significant at 5% level

points we have substantial evidence of randomness, but the evidence is not universal.

Next let's turn to the yields themselves, which, in our earlier analysis, correspond to the exponents of cumulated ran-

dom variables. These data are given in Table 25.4. Again, the
cases where the series fails the randomness test are noted by
an asterisk(*). In every case, the actual yield series was not
random. Thus, while the differences in the logs of yields were
random, the yields themselves were not. Runs tests produced
essentially the same result.

Table 25.4 Turning Points of Selected Yields

Maturity	Actual Turns	Expected Turns	Probability of Difference
U.S. Government Yields, 1950–1986			
3 month	204	290	.00*
1 year	186	290	.00*
2 years	188	290	.00*
5 years	184	290	.00*
10 years	202	290	.00*
20 years	202	290	.00*
Durand Corporate 1900–1965			
1 year	36	42.7	.048*
5 years	34	42.7	.01*
10 years	34	42.7	.01*
15 years	36	42.7	.048*
20 years	34	42.7	.01*
25 years	30	42.7	.00*
30 years	28	42.7	.00*
Macaulay 1857–1936/7			
Commercial Paper	376	639.3	.00*
Long Corporate	330	636.7	.00*
British Consol 1730–1961	102	153	.00*
S&P Long 1900–79	334	637.3	.00*

*Significant at 5% level

Conclusion

Evidence on runs indicates the following:

1. For the most part, first differences in the logs of yields are random.
2. The yields themselves are not random.
3. Changes in yields are not random.
4. This evidence supplements the evidence from the signs tests, confirming that changes in the logs of interest rates are random.

CHAPTER 26

Signed Rankings

O ur previous two tests of randomness were both non-parametric and fairly simple. One test observed the number of increases and decreases; the other observed the number of runs. In each case, we found substantial but not unanimous evidence of randomness. For some series in some periods, we found differences between changes in interest rates and a purely random series.

Neither the signs test nor the runs test took account of the magnitude of changes in interest rates or the magnitude of changes in the logarithms of interest rates, our primary variable. In this chapter, we wish to look not at the actual magnitude of changes but at the rankings of the magnitudes. This type of test is different than the other two in that it takes account of the ordinal rankings, as well as the signs of change. It shows whether the ranked magnitudes of the series, above and below the median, are similar. So it is, in a sense, a measure of symmetry and a nonparametric measure not dependent on the underlying distribution of the data.

This test is known as the *Wilcox signed ranks test* applied to a single sample. It determines whether the median of change in rates is different than zero or than any other given value. It also measures the degree of similarity of increases and decreases by examining the average ranks of each. If the distributions of positive and negative changes are symmetric, the average ranks will be the same. If we are interested in increases and decreases in a series whose mean change (or median change) is expected to be zero and the probability of an increase of any given magnitude is the same as the probability of a similar decrease, then the average rank of decreases (as opposed to the average value of the decreases) should be equal to the average rank of increases. This would hold in the long run for large samples, but it would not be true where all increases were of large magnitude and all decreases of small magnitude, or vice verse (i.e. if all increases were of small magnitude and all decreases of large magnitude). So the calculation of average rank gives some measure of the symmetry between positive and negative changes.

We illustrate the Wilcox signed ranks test using the following series:

$$-9 \ -7 \ -3 \ -1 \ 0 \ 2 \ 5 \ 6 \ 8$$

We find the median value (0) and subtract it then from each item in the series. In this case, we get the same series (-9 -7 -3 -1 0 2 5 6 8), since the median is 0. Now, we rank the series in ascending order of absolute value, dropping the median figure. The ranking is:

$$0 \ -1 \ 2 \ -3 \ 5 \ 6 \ -7 \ 8 \ -9$$

The signed ranks of these numbers are:

$$1^* \ -2 \ 3 \ -4 \ 5 \ 6 \ -7 \ 8 \ -9$$

Next, we add up the ranks of the negative figures, and we add up the ranks of the positive figures. In this case, the sum of the negative ranks is 22 and the sum of the positive ranks is 22. We exclude the rank of the median figure (0) whose rank 1 is shown with an asterisk.

The expected value of the rank of each size is $n \ (n +1)/4$. In this example, that calculation gives $(9 \ (9 + 1))/4 = 22.5$. Thus, the expected and actual values are very close. The variance of the expected value is given by the equation $s^2 = n(n+1)(2n+1)/24$. The standard deviation is the square root of that. In the above case, we have the following variance:

$$s^2 = 9(10)(19)/24 = 8.1$$

For large samples, we can test for real differences between the estimated figure and the mean by finding $z = x/s$. In this case, we have $z = 0.5/8.1 = 0.06$. The probability of getting a z of 0.06 or greater is very high. Thus, in this hypothetical case, where n is too small for a proper z-test, we conclude that the series is random.

Next, let's run these tests on the first difference in the logs of the interest rate series. The rankings are the same as those given by simple first differences in interest rates. We can run the tests in two ways: first, against a hypothesized mean of zero, and second, against the actual mean, which was never more than 0.01. The first test shows whether the mean is significantly different than zero. The second test shows whether the actual median was the right one and also gives us a measure of the equality of the rankings of the changes above and below the median. Let's start with the first test which is a test of a median of zero. See Table 26.1.

Most of the series where n is large are significantly different than zero at the 0.05 level. But, as you can see, the average rankings of increases and decreases are not very far apart, within 10% of each other, generally. In the longest series, the average rankings of increases and decreases are not different than those in a random series.

Next let's look at the average rankings around the actual median in Table 26.2. This time we get a quite different result. All of the series, but one, show very similar average ranks, sufficiently similar for the difference not to be statistically significant. This is clear evidence that the rankings above and below median are similar. In addition, the sums are random.

Table 26.1   Signed Rankings of First Differences in Logs of Yields Based on Median of Zero

	Average Negative Rank	Average Positive Rank	Probabililty of Difference
U.S. Government Yields 1950–1986			
3 months	219	224	.01*
1 year	221	222	.04*
2 years	228	216	.05
5 years	235	220	.02*
10 years	234	222	.00*
20 years	245	227	.01*
Durand Corporate 1900–1965			
1 year	35	34	.64
5 years	32	36	.84
10 years	33	36	.84
15 years	34	34	.89
20 years	33	35	.82
25 years	34	34	.93
30 years	35	36	.99
Macaulay 1857–1936/7			
Comm. Paper	533	509	.18
Long Corporate	533	502	.00*
British Consol 1730–1961	120	122	.43
S&P Long 1900–1979	527	546	.08

*Significant at 5% level

Table 26.2   Signed Rankings of First Differences in Logs of Yields Based on Actual Median

	Average Negative Rank	Average Positive Rank	Probabililty of Difference
U.S. Government Yields 1950–1986			
3 months	215	224	.69
1 year	233	206	.25
2 years	227	212	.54
5 years	222	217	.85
10 years	228	211	.47
20 years	220	219	.93
Durand Corporate 1900–1965			
1 year	33	34	.90
5 years	29	36	.40
10 years	33	36	.84
15 years	34	34	.89
20 years	33	35	.82
25 years	34	34	.93
30 years	35	36	.99
Macaulay 1857–1936/7			
Comm. Paper	533	509	.18
Long Corporate	533	502	.00[*]
British Consol 1730–1961	115	118	.85
S&P Long 1900–1979	527	545	.08

[*]Significant at 5% level

Conclusion

1. The signed rank tests show that the distributions
    were symmetric with respect to the median for all
    series and with respect to zero for most. This repre-
    sents further evidence of randomness.

CHAPTER 27

Autocorrelation of Interest Rates and Changes in Interest Rates

Next, we turn to the topic of autocorrelation. Is the series of interest rates correlated with itself in the sense that successive elements of the series are related to each other? If autocorrelation is present, then the items in a series are correlated or related to each other over time.

In using autocorrelation, we compute the coefficient of correlation between each item in the series and items k units apart. The variable k is the lag, a quantity vary can vary from zero to some number less than the number of items in the series. When the lag is zero, we find the correlation between each item in the series and itself; that is, we correlate the series with itself. The coefficient of correlation is therefore 1.0, indicating perfect correlation. When the lag is 1, we correlate each item in the series with the adjacent item. When the lag is 2, we correlate each item with the item two units away.

How the coefficient of correlation changes as we increase the lag tells us a great deal about the series. When we perform autocorrelation on the set of integers, the coefficient of correlation is 1 for all lags. For any series whose first differences are a constant, we will obtain coefficients of 1 for all lags. For a harmonic series, such as a sine series, we will get a series of coefficients whose values decline monotonically from 1 at lag zero to 0 and then rise monotonically to 1 and decline monotonically again to 0, and so on.

The interval between perfect correlations is constant, and we can see the periodicity of the series in that of the coefficients of autocorrelation. For a random series, there will be no correlation between successive items in the series, except at lag 1, where the correlation will be perfect. For a series formed by cumulating random elements, which we seem to have for bond yields, the coefficients of autocorrelation for the yield series will begin at 1 at lag 0 and decline monotonically to zero. First differences in such a series, or in log first differences, the coefficient of autocorrelation at lag 0 will be 1 and zero thereafter. If our model is only approximately correct, we will get approximately these results.

We can examine autocorrelation in several ways: (1) by looking at the original series itself, (2) by looking at the logs of the series, (3) by looking at first differences in the series, or 4) by looking at first differences in the logs of the series. We will look at the original series and at first differences in the logs of the original series.

What we expect depends on what kind of series we think we have. We believe that the first difference in the logs of the yields are an approximately random series. In that case we would expect zero correlation for the first difference in the logs series, except at lag 0. For the yield series itself, we would expect the correlation coefficient to drop from 1 at lag 0 to a very low value at a long lag.

Figure 27.1 gives the autocorrelation functions of six yield series: U.S. 3-month, 1950 to 1986 monthly; U.S 20 year, 1950 to 1986 monthly, commercial paper and long corporate 1857 to 1936/1937, monthly; and 6.125 short bonds and 8.25 long bonds, 1987, daily. Note how the coefficient drops from 1 at lag 0 to low coefficients at higher lags. For the Macaulay commercial paper series, the coefficient becomes insignificant at about lag 50 and close to zero by lag 180. The apparent periodicity in that series of coefficients is interesting.

Figure 27.1 Estimated Autocorrelation of Yields, Selected Yield Series

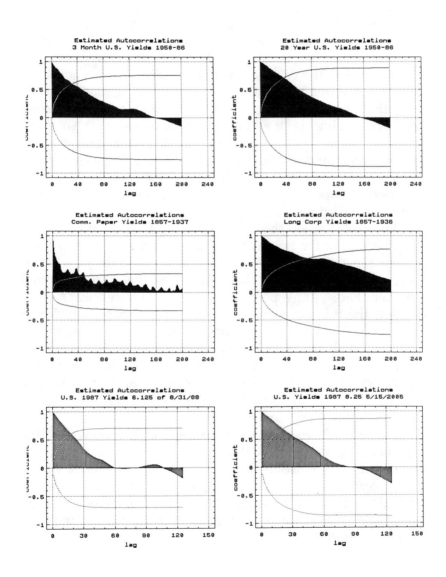

All six series reflect the behavior of data whose differences are random. The coefficients of autocorrelation begin at 1 at lag 0 and decline toward zero at longer lags. The hyperbolic line on each panel of the figure gives the significance level at two standard deviations. The coefficients of autocorrelation become insignificant between lags 20 and 40 for all series except the long corporate yields, where the lag is approximately 70 months. For the commercial paper series, there is some periodicity at about 12 months. For cumulants of random numbers, the figure would portray a monotonically decreasing line. The decline in the coefficients indicates that we have neither a linear series nor a periodic series but a series formed by summing random elements. All six figures have roughly the same pattern, perhaps with the exception of the Macaulay commercial paper (graph C), which exhibits the same decline in the coefficient with increases in the lag.

Figure 27.2 gives the coefficients of autocorrelation for the same series but for first differences in the series. Autocorrelation of the first differences will reveal two things: whether there is any correlation in differences over any lag and whether there is any periodicity in first differences. As you can see, there is no significant autocorrelation for any lag in any graph. All of the coefficients are low, generally below 0.15 or 0.10, and all are insignificant. Moreover, the coefficients are negative as often as they are positive. Except for the commercial paper yields (graph C), there doesn't appear to be any periodicity in the coefficients. In the commercial paper series, some periodicity appears at annual intervals.

Figure 27.3 gives the autocorrelation functions for first differences in the natural logarithms of the same series. The results are very close to those of the first differences, except for the commercial paper series (graph C), where the apparent periodicity is even stronger. Again, the coefficients are all below 0.15, except for the commercial paper yields, and thus are rarely significant.

Figure 27.2 Estimated Autocorrelation of First Differences in Yields, Selected Yield Series

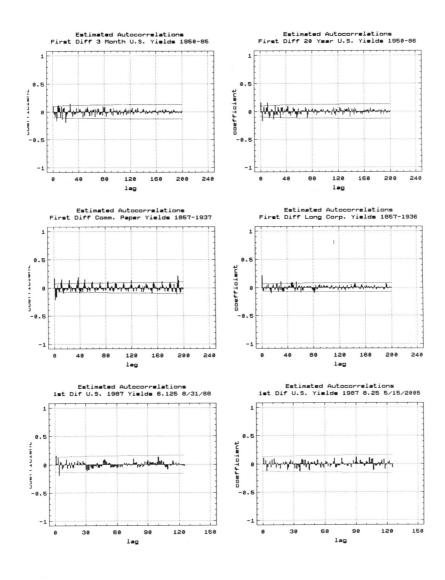

Figure 27.3 Estimated Autocorrelation of First Differences in Logarithms of Yields, Selected Yield Series

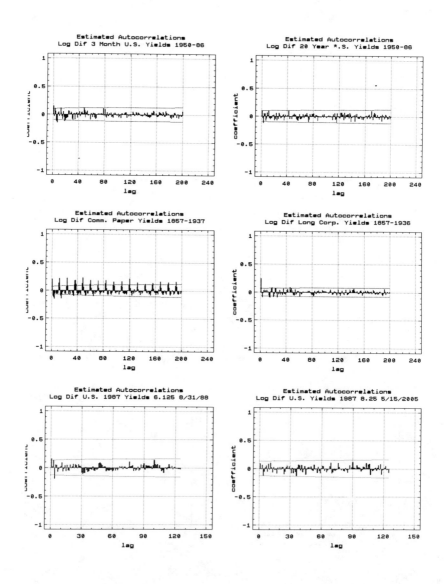

Conclusion

1. For yields, the coefficients of autocorrelation decline slowly, reaching zero for the monthly series after a decade or two.
2. For first differences in yields, the coefficients of autocorrelation are generally not significant after lag 0, indicating randomness.
3. For first differences in the logarithms of yields, the coefficients of autocorrelation is not significant after lag 0.
4. The lack of autocorrelation for changes in yields is indicative of randomness.

CHAPTER 28

Spectral Analysis

A common way of analyzing time-series data is by estimating a frequency spectrum, which allows you to decompose the variance of the data into contributions over a range of frequencies. Such an analysis is based on representing the series as a sum of sinusoids at the Fourier frequencies.

Figure 28.1 gives the periodogram of yields for six monthly series. The analysis is based on representing the series as a sum of sinusoids at the Fourier frequencies. We plot the squared amplitudes of the sinusoids. The graphs are scaled such that if the mean of the series is zero, the sum of the periodogram ordinates equals the sum of the squared data values. The figure reveals no periodicty in the series.

Figure 28.2 gives the ordinates in logs. Again, there appears to be very little periodicity in any of the graphs. A series which had, say, a 12-month cycle would show a peak at regular 12-month intervals. That is clearly not the case here.

Figure 28.3 presents an integrated periodogram, a kind of figure that verifies whether the time series is random. In each graph, the cumulative sums of the periodogram ordinates are plotted normalized to a 0.1 vertical scale. Each graph includes the 75% and 95% Kolmogorov-Smirnov bounds for a uniform distribution of ordinates. We plot the first differences in the natural logarithms of the original yield series rather than the original series. For graphs A, B, E, and F, the series are clearly

Figure 28.1 Periodogram, Arithmetic Ordinate, Selected Yield Series

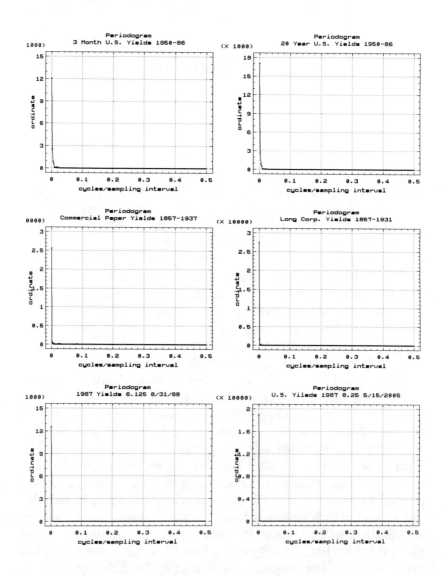

Figure 28.2 Periodogram, Log Ordinate, Selected Yield Series

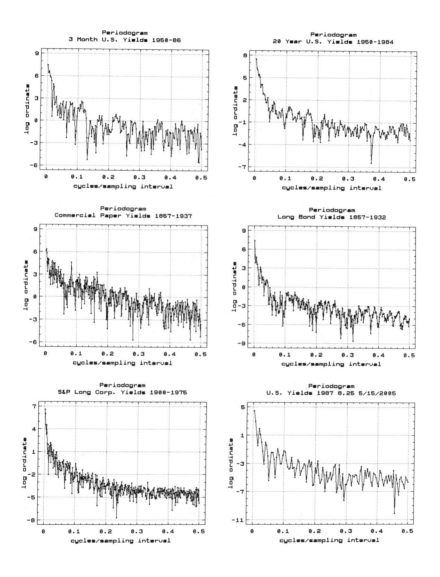

Figure 28.3 Integrated Periodogram, Selected Yield Series

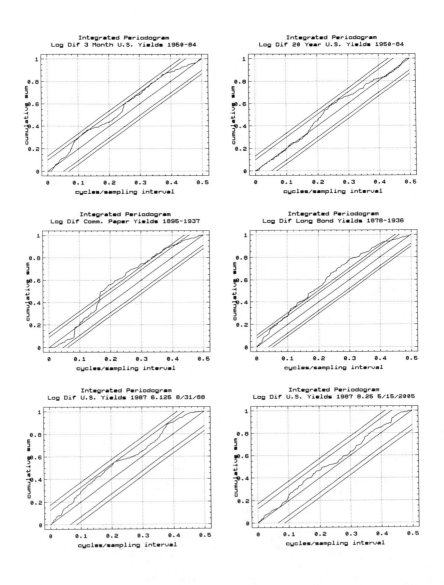

random, since the points lay within the Kolmogorov-Smirnov 95% bounds. That is not true for the two Macaulay series, graphs C and D, which reveal some nonrandomness.

Figure 28.4 is a seasonal subseries plot of the same yield data, which will reveal any seasonal pattern to the data, if one exists. All of the data for a single month are plotted in the same panel. That is to say, all of the January data are plotted on the far (0-1) left and all the December data are plotted on the far right (11-12). If there is a seasonal component, the monthly means (indicated by the lines for each month) will be different. Note that, in the figure, the means for every series except the commercial paper series are the same every month. From this, we can deduce that there is no seasonal component in the data. For the commercial paper series, there is a slightly higher mean for the latter months of the year, indicating very slight seasonality.

Conclusion

1. Based on periodogram analysis, there appear to be no significant periodicity in the yield series or in first differences in the logs of yields, the only exception being some departures for the 1857 to 1936 data.
2. The plot of seasonality reveals no significant seasonality.

Figure 28.4 Seasonal Subseries Plot, Selected Yield Series

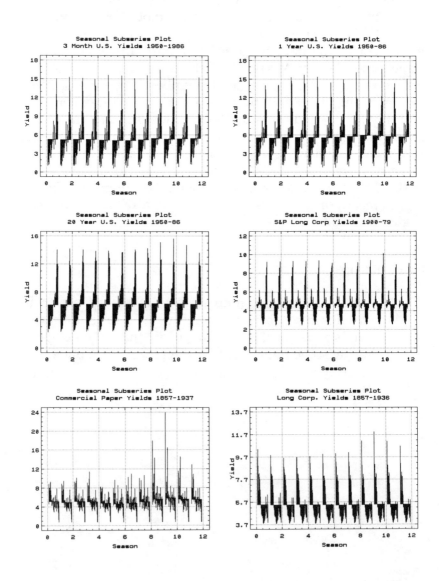

CHAPTER 29

Short-Term Forecasting of Interest Rates

In previous chapters we have suggested that changes in interest rates resemble a random walk. If this model is correct, then we cannot make accurate forecasts of future rates.

Since World War II, particularly within the past decade, a number of short-term forecasting techniques have been developed and applied to many economic time series, including interest rates. These techniques include econometric models, filter models, autoregression and moving average models (ARIMA), decomposition techniques, and exponential smoothing models. Many of these techniques have been incorporated in micro computer software and applied by bankers, brokerage firms, investment firms, and government entities for trading, investment, and analytical purposes. If these models are able to predict long-term or even short term interest rates, then the random walk model which we have suggested is not the correct model.

There is a clear conflict between the view that time series forecasting models can forecast interest rates and the view that interest rates are largely a random walk. Only one of the views is correct, not both. How can we resolve this conflict. One way is to test the models to determine whether they produce accurate predictions. Another way is to attempt to assess the general method and assumptions of the models to determine whether they are likely to work if it is true that interest rates are a random walk.

Unfortunately, we do not know to what extent forecasting models are being applied to interest rates or how well they work. We know that some models are being used by some banks to forecast rates, but the forecasts are limited to one week in advance. Thus, our knowledge of the use and accuracy of interest rate forecasting is limited.

We can turn to the second alternative. In assessing the general method and assumptions of forecasting models, it is helpful to examine their history. There are two historical origins of time series analysis, one initiated by Bachelier in 1900, the other by Yule in the 1930's. Bachelier attempted to describe mathematically short-term interest rates and from his description he derived the random walk model which he related to games of chance. Yule, on the other hand, attempted to forecast various economic series using autoregressive schemes. What Yule did with his data Bachelier would not have considered doing with his. Yule looked for trends and cycles, Bachelier for the underlying characteristics of the series. Thus, at the very beginning of time series analysis, there was a dichotomy in approach. This dichotomy is at the heart of the conflict described here and is of fundamental importance.

Bachelier's approach was that the series is approximately a random walk of zero mean and constant variance. The distribution of changes in the series is a normal distribution of independent variables of zero mean. In fact, as we have seen, the mean is not always zero, the variance is not constant, the distribution not normal, and therefore the random walk model is only an approximation. In the interest rates series there is some nonstationarity of means and variances, but the underlying series is essentially a random walk.

It is a surprising fact that a random walk exhibits what appear to be remarkably like trends and cycles, not regular trends and cycles, but trends and cycles of unpredictable length and direction. The presence of trends and cycles in purely random series was suggested by Roberts in his simulation of the stock market; the same presence of trends and cycles is pointed out by Feller in illustrations in his work on probability.

Although Yule was a statistician, he approached the problem of analyzing economic time series in a very different way from Bachelier. He approached it in the way an engineer would and quickly applied an autoregressive scheme. Most of his successors in forecasting were engineers who approached the problem of forecasting in the same way. Weiner, Box, Jenkins, Kalman, Brown, were all engineers by training, they all viewed the world from an engineering perspective, and they all used engineering terms to describe their work. An engineer sees processes as a regularity upon which is imposed a set of errors. The errors may be actual error, observational error, or both, but they are errors to the process, not the central part of it. The basic form of most physical processes, such as the path of a rocket in space, can be modeled by a simple autoregression equation of the form:

$$y\ (t) = a\ (1)\ y\ (t-1) + a\ (2)\ y\ (t-2) + ... + a\ (n)\ y\ (t-n) + e\ (t).$$

This autoregressive model was the model used by Yule, and it is the foundation of many forecasting schemes. The left hand variable of the autoregression equation, $y\ (t)$ is the present position of the rocket. All the right hand variables of the equation, $y\ (t-1)$, $y\ (t-2)$, etc., except the last, are the values of the series $y\ (t)$ at times $t-1$, $t-2$, etc. They are the previous positions of the rocket, for example. The far right hand element of the equation, $e\ (t)$ is the error term. Errors are always present in the measurement and observation of any physical system, but they are random and unpredictable. More important, in a physical process the errors are generally minor in relation to the process itself, the general course of the rocket through space.

When the engineer looks at the world in this way, he sees the task of forecasting as the extraction of the underlying process. He wants to identify the underlying autoregressive process, or the moving average process, by removing the error and leaving only the process, or the regularity in the system. The process is modeled by the coefficients of the autoregressive equation, a (1), a (2), etc. Once we have the process, or the coefficients of the equation, we can predict the future from the past.

In making forecasts, we are subject, of course, to the inevitable but small error. The error is considered to be small by engineers because in most physical processes the error is small. That the error is considered small is reflected in name engineers have given it—they call it "noise." The word noise suggests something minor, an interruption, a small shock to the system. The word noise suggests the engineers view of economic time series wherein the regularity is what we look for by removing the errors. In Bachelier's view, on the other hand, the error is all there is. No regularity is present.

By applying to the data a filter or other technique, the engineer filters out the noise and extract the underlying process and uses the model of that process to predict its future, just as he would if he were given the observed series of positions of a rocket, clouded by actual and observational errors. Once he had removed those errors, he can model the past positions of the rocket and forecast where it will be in the future.

Clearly these two viewpoints of the economic world are in conflict. One says there is a regularity plus random elements; the other says there is nothing regular, only the random element. At the extremes, these two viewpoints are very different. In practice, their differences may be less. The differences lie in the relative magnitude of the regular element and the random element. As the former shrinks and the latter becomes predominant, the series becomes increasingly random and vice versa.

The issue for any particular series is where the division lies between regularity and randomness. Bachelier would say that the interest rate series is entirely random, all noise. Yule might say that it is primarily regularity. The modern forecaster might say that even though the process is largely random, we can still model it using new more powerful techniques. The belief that even largely random processes can be modeled and predicted adds a third complication to the question of forecasting interest rates.

Let us turn to the accuracy of the models using a slightly wider perspective than simply asking how well the forecasts work. From a wider perspective, the question of how well the forecast models work falls into three parts. First, how well does the model fits past data? Second, how well the model fitted to past data forecasts future data? Third, does the fit to past data bears any relationship to the ability to forecast future data? To put the last question in slightly different form, does finding that a model very closely, or even exactly, fits past data mean that the model will also closely forecast future data. This last part of the issue is important because time series forecasters typically select models not on the basis of how well they might fit the future, but rather on the basis of how well they fit the past. If there is no relationship between past fit and future accuracy, the method of selecting models commonly employed is inappropriate.

The answer to the last question gives us some clue as to the answers to the first two questions. Surprisingly, modern forecasting models are able to fit almost perfectly the past values a random walk. A random walk, by definition, is a series whose precise future values are unpredictable. That means that modern models can closely fit the past values of an unpredictable series. Getting a nearly perfect fit to a random walk is no mean achievement. But if we can fit a model to an unpredictable series, what then is the relevance of good fits to forecasting accuracy? It certainly suggests that past fit is not necessarily a good clue to future accuracy. This is an important point. It also means that the extensive effort done to find models that fit well may be wasted effort if the goal is accurate forecasts. Finally, it means that we may not be able to use the goodness of fit to the past as a guide to accuracy of the forecast.

This bleak assessment of past fit's relevance to future forecasts is borne out by the evidence. The evidence for large numbers of varied economic time series is that good fits are not related to good forecasts, or vice versa. Past fit is not a good proxy for future fit for many types of economic series. There is simply no relationship in general for wildly varying economic series between the past fit of the model and the accuracy of the forecasts made by that model. Somewhat ironically, the evidence reveals that the very methods used to chose models for forecasting are not the methods that will ensure forecast accuracy. The models with the best statistical scores are not much better in making forecasts than the models with the worst statistical scores. That is the general result, though it will certainly differ for different economic series and will certainly not be true of certain series.

Forecasting models work very well, however, in forecasting certain kinds of data. They work well with airline passenger miles, with electricity sales, with certain types of production processes. They probably work well because they are able to fit a pattern which repeats itself on a daily or monthly basis, or year after year. The airline traffic series and the demand for electricity are good examples of such series because the pattern, which in any cycle may be partly random, repeats itself period after period. By applying decomposition, autoregression moving averages, or exponential smoothing, these patterns can be modeled very well. We know that they should be able to be modeled because we know there should be an underlying cycle and we see the cycle in the data. But when the process may be purely random, when we do not see any clear evidence of cycles of constant length periods, then we have no basis for presuming that a regularity exists and we may have a simple random walk.

But the high degree of explanation of past data, which is suggested by the equations and in the autoregressive moving average models and in other techniques for interest rates, is also found in the simple autoregressive equation $y(t) = y(t) + e(t)$ which is the equation for a random walk.

In a random walk, the probability of making an exact replication declines with n so that after n future steps, the probability of exact replication is $1/n$. The standard deviation of the future position of the walk is the square root of n, which enables us to calculate the probability of being at any distance from the present level, but not precisely where.

What can we conclude? We can conclude that forecasting models will probably not work on interest rates because interest rates are largely a random walk. There must be some form of regularity, either a trend, a cycle, or seasonality which is part of the process in order to make predictions of changes in the future that are better than the flip of a coin. This assertion is restricted to univariate prediction, or prediction of the future interest rate series from past values of the same series. The series could be a random walk and still be related to something else, but that is a different matter.

Conclusion

1. Modern forecasting models are able to fit the past values of unpredictable series (random walks) almost perfectly.

2. How well a model fits past data is not a sufficient criteria of future forecasting accuracy for interest rate series. For economic series in general, how well the model fits past data is not related to how well the model forecasts the future. Other criteria are necessary.

3. There must be some form of regularity in a series, periodic or cyclic, seasonal, or trend, to allow accurate forecasts. Without such regularity, it is not possible to forecast changes in the series with any accuracy.

4. The models that have provided the best fits to past interest data are autoregressive schemes which are, or are very close to, random walk models [ARIMA(1,1,0)]. This closeness is not only evidence for the random walk model, but evidence for the inability to forecast future rates.

CHAPTER 30

Interest Rates and Inflation

In the previous chapters of this book, we have not considered the relationship between interest rates and other economic variables. The reason for this exclusion was partly that we wanted to examine interest rates as a time series in its own right. While it may be true that interest rates may have fundamental relationships to other variables, the random character of interest rates makes this unlikely.

If any series has a relationship to interest rates, the best possible candidate is the consumer price index. It is widely believed that when inflation is high, bond interest rates should also be high to offset the loss of real value on coupons and principal repayments in future years.

In an attempt to examine the relationship between inflation and interest rates, we have selected two sets of yield and inflation series. The first set is the annual British consol yield and the British wholesale price index from 1750 to 1961. While we would have preferred a consumer price index, none is available for this long historical period so we use the wholesale index instead. For the recent period, we compare the U.S. consumer price index with 3-month U.S. treasury yields from 1950 to 1986, using monthly data for both series.

Before looking at the data, it is important to note that a price index and an interest rate series are different kinds of series. A price index is an average of individual series which probably have considerable cross-sectional dispersion. If the underlying series are random walks in their logarithms, then the composite price series will have an upward drift. If these series are like the stock market, then that drift will be about 5% per year. What the precise drift is depends on the cross-sectional standard deviation of the individual series and on whether they are random walks in their logarithms. The interest rate series are not averages and are not computed in the manner the consumer or wholesale price indexes are. Moreover, their cross-sectional dispersion is quite small. As a result interest rate series do not have the upward drift that price indexes have. Consequently, the inflation and yield series are quite different series.

Our method of analysis is to examine the ratio of the bond yield to the price index. The data for the British long term yield/wholesale prices is given in Figure 30.1. Graphs A and B give the ratio itself and first differences in the natural logarithms of the ratio. As you can see, the ratio looks like a typical interest rate series and the first differences in the logs looks like a similar graph of an interest rate series. Graph D gives the autocorrelation function and reveals no significant autocorrelation. Graph E shows that the frequency distribution of changes in the natural logarithms of the ratio is bell shaped with about as many increases as decreases. Graph F demonstrates that the standard deviation of changes in the ratio rises with the square root of the difference interval.

All of this data suggests that the ratio of yields to prices is a random variable, a quantity that reveals no relationship over the long run between the price index and long-term interest rates. In Graph C of Figure 30.1 we show the two series as indexes with the 1750 value set at 1.0 for both yields and wholesale prices. Overall, there doesn't appear to be much relationship between the two series. By 1961 wholesale prices had climbed to over six times their initial value whereas interest rates had only doubled. Thus, wholesale prices were much more volatile.

The next figure, Figure 30.2, shows the same data for the ratio of 3-month yields to consumer prices from 1950 to 1986. Again, the yield/price series looks like an interest rates series

Figure 30.1 British Consol Yields/Wholesale Prices, 1750–1961

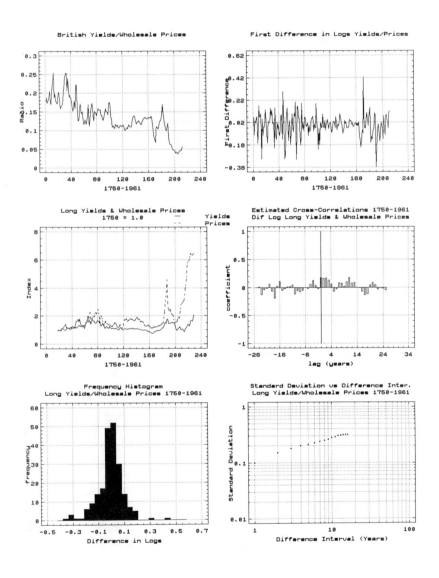

Figure 30.2 3-Month U.S. Yields/Consumer Prices, 1950–1986

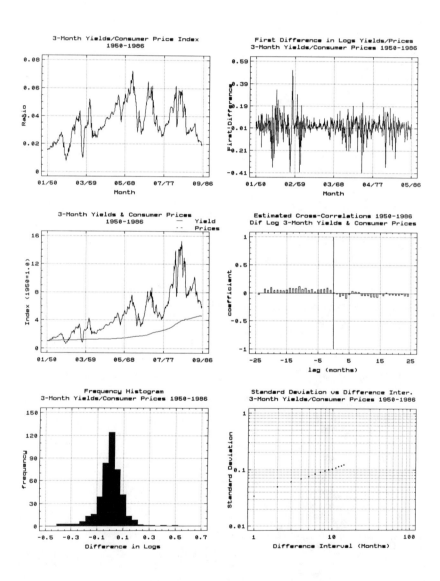

(Graph A); the first differences in the logs are chaotic (Graph B); there is no significant autocorrelation (Graph D); the histogram of first differences in the natural logarithms is bell-shaped and records about as many increases as decreases (Graph E); and the standard deviation of differences in the natural logarithms rises with the square root of the difference interval (Graph F). All of these graphs suggest a ratio series that is a random walk. Graph C of the two indexes shows a fairly steady consumer price index against a highly volatile 3-month yield series. It shows that the volatility in the ratio is caused, not by changes in consumer prices, but by the volatility of 3-month interest rates.

In order to bring the impact of interest rates out more clearly, we show in Figure 30.3 data for the consumer price index alone. Graph A shows the index, a rising line that does not look like a random walk. A graph of the logarithms of the series (not shown) reveals a much more consistent rate of rise. Graph B of first differences in the logarithms shows that there is a marked upward drift, despite a lot of volatility. The integrated periodogram of first differences in the logarithms reveals a nonrandom series since the graph is well outside two standard deviations. The estimated autocorrelations of first differences in the logs (Graph D) reveals significant autocorrelation for lags up to 20 months. Graph E for first differences in the logarithms reveals a distribution skewed to the right, most changes considerably greater than zero. The standard deviation of changes in the logarithms does rise with the difference interval (Graph F). Only Graph E suggests a random walk. All other graphs all reveal a series that has a strong upward drift wherein the random component is too small in comparison to the upward drift to reveal a random walk. This consumer price index is definitely not random.

Conclusion

1. The ratio of interest rates to wholesale prices is a random walk based on 1750 to 1961 British annual data.

Figure 30.3 Consumer Price Index, 1950–1986

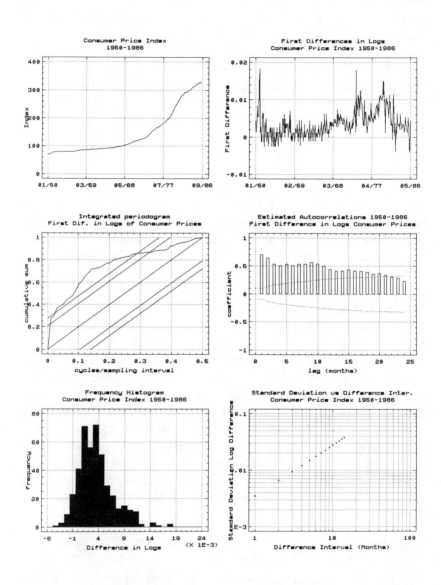

2. The ratio of short-term interest rates to the consumer price index is a random walk, based on U.S. 1950 to 1986 monthly data.

3. The U.S. consumer price index is not a random walk over the 1950 to 1986 period.

4. Since the ratio of interest rates to wholesale and consumer prices appears to be a random walk, there doesn't appear to be much relationship between interest rates and inflation.

CHAPTER 31

Summary

We have looked interest rate data and some bond-price data from many perspectives in an attempt to understand the underlying process that may generate the series. We have broken down the original data, taken differences in reported yields and compiled yield indexes, computed the logs of these series, and found the first differences in the logs. We have plotted the distributions of these data, examined their standard deviations and semi-intersextile ranges, and studied how these measures both rise with increases in the difference interval (roughly with the square root of the length of that interval), a rate of dispersion characteristic of Brownian motion.

Changes in yield series seem chaotic, whether measured by the original series or by the logs of the original series. The distribution of log changes is roughly normal, with more large and small changes than occur in a Gaussian distribution.

The absolute degree of change measured by the standard deviation is generally higher for long than for short maturities; for yield indexes, this is nearly always so but not for individual issues. These characteristics apply to many different historical eras, extending back to the eighteenth century for the British consol series, the nineteenth century Macaulay data, and the twentieth century Durand corporate data and Salomon U.S. government data.

The statistical characteristics of interest rates are not entirely invariant over all historical eras. The standard deviation of changes in the logs of rates, while generally within the same rough bounds, is sometimes much higher, sometimes much lower. The historical era seems to be more important than the type issue, government or corporate, in determining the level of volatility of changes in rates or the precise form of the distribution.

The most pronounced characteristic of interest rates, is their tendency to move together. However, the standard deviation of changes in rates varied among different maturities in the same period. In the 1950 to 1986 period, short-term rates were most volatile in the first decade, long-term rates in the last decade when rate changes were measured in logs.

The slope of the yield curve fluctuates at random, with rises and falls in the slope and changes in direction occurring unpredictably. Since short rates are much more volatile than long rates, most of the changes in the slope of yield curve resulted from changes in short-term rates. There is little evidence of any lead-lag relationship between changes in short-term and changes in long-term rates. There is no inherent upward bias in interest rates like there is in common stock averages.

The nearly equal proportion of increases and decreases in rates at all yield levels indicates that there is no tendency for rates to revert to a mean or normal value. The sequences of positive and negative changes were the same kinds of sequences we would get from flipping coins or a random drawing of equal proportions of positive and negative integers. The examination of runs and turning points both suggested randomness.

The process generating interest rates has all the hallmarks of a random process. That is, the series looks like the logs of interest rates; the exponents of that series look like the interest rate series itself; and first differences in the logs of interest rates look like differences in the running sum of coin flips, albeit with some important differences (mainly wider tails and a thinner girth in the distribution).

Unlike the stock market average (which has an upward bias due to the act of averaging a series of random walks, each of which has an approximately lognormal distribution), there is no inherent upward bias in interest rates due to the mathematical nature of the process itself. We found no tendency for rates to revert to a mean, based on the lack of evidence that decreases in rates occur more frequently than increases when rates are high, or vice versa. The interest rates series seems unaffected by any evidence of the mean-reverting tendency that characterizes some forms of Brownian motion.

Although our investigation of bond prices was limited, the limited evidence did show that the price series was the mirror of the interest rates series for the same bond and that all of the characteristics of interest rates held for prices. Changes in prices were random, with a standard deviation that increases with the square root of the difference interval, an approximately normal distribution, and past changes giving no indication of future changes. This is true of a bond not close to maturity, since at that time, its price as well as its yield will approach the coupon yield and the par value. For a perpetuity, certainly, the form of the statistical characteristics is identical.

How can we summarize? Interest rate series, as reflected in first differences in the logs, behave like random processes. Past changes in the series give no indication of future changes with respect to particular magnitude or direction, except in a probabilistic sense. We can't predict with more than a 50% probability whether future rates will rise or fall. We can however, predict the probability distribution of changes in general over any time period, since the spread of the probable distribution, measured by the standard deviation, increases with the square root of the forecast interval. Our forecast of the probable distribution will not be perfect, since standard deviations do change somewhat from period to period.

The expected mean change in rates is zero generally speaking, and there appear to be no or at least very few trends that are statistically significant. Nor is there any tendency to return to former levels; just because rates have fallen doesn't mean that they will rise, or vice versa.

While the yield curve does tend to smooth, it seems an arbitrary result of random changes. Nonetheless, if there is anything resembling equilibrium in interest rates, it is this smoothing of the yield curve. Beyond that, the concept of equilibrium seems to have to basis in fact, for how can something that changes at random be deemed in any sense to approach or be in equilibrium?

In conclusion, the interest rate series appear to be a random walk with an approximately lognormal distribution, a form of Brownian motion.

Appendix: Summary of Chapter Conclusions

Interest Rates and their Transformations

Chapter 2   The Record of Interest Rates

There are at least four characteristics of interest rates:

1. Yields exhibit continuous fluctuation.
2. There appears to be a great deal of comovement among different maturities in the same historical period.
3. In some series, the degree of fluctuation appears to be related to the level of rates.
4. The degree of fluctuation seems to be inversely related to the maturity of the bond.

Although we did see evidence of a trend in some groups of series, we did not in others, which suggests that, while trends may be present, they are definitely not universal.

Chapter 3   Changes in Interest Rates

First differences in interest rates have the following characteristics:

1. Volatility of change in interest rates characterizes all periods but seems to differ somewhat from one period to the next.
2. Volatility is higher when yields are higher.
3. Yields of long bonds are less volatile than yields of short bonds.
4. The pattern of volatility in the same historical period is similar for all maturities.
5. There appear to be as many increases as decreases in yield.
6. The magnitude of increases and decreases is similar in any given period.

Chapter 4   Logs of Interest Rates

Any series of yields for a particular bond may be transformed into the logs of yields and the logs of yields can, by the inverse transformation, be converted back to the original yields.

1. The log transformation is important because it converts a yield series whose degree of fluctuation (or variance) is much higher when yields are high than when they are low into a series whose volatility is not dependent on the level of yields.
2. When we remove the arbitrary effect of level of yield from the interest rates series, we obtain a graph of yields which reveals a pattern quite different from that of the graph of the original yields.
3. The degree of fluctuation in the logs of yields appears to be more equal over time.
4. The sharp changes in volatility that had appeared in the original yield series are now seen to be largely a function of scale, or of the level of yields.

Chapter 5   Changes in the Logs of Interest Rates

1. Scale has an impact on volatility, and measurement in logs removes this.

2. All series are highly volatile and the nature of the volatility (but not the degree) is similar for all maturities and all time periods.
3. Volatility is not the same in all historical periods.
4. The volatility pattern in the same historical period is similar for all maturities.
5. Short maturities are much more volatile than long maturities.
6. Past changes cannot be used to predict whether future changes will be positive or negative.
7. The numbers of positive and negative changes appear to be approximately equal.
8. There are more small than large changes.

Chapter 6   *How the Level of Interest Rates Affects*
           Interest Rate Volatility

Based on the evidence of the relationship between the level of yields and the standard deviation of changes in yields and the standard deviation of changes in the logs of yields, we may conclude:

1. The degree of change in yields, or the volatility of yields, is directly related to the level of yields.
2. The degree of change in the logs of yields is not related to the level of yields.
3. We can homogenize interest rate data by transforming yields into the their logs and thereby obtain a series whose variance is more stationary.
4. In analyzing the underlying characteristics of interest rates, the logs of the series should be used, otherwise the results will be affected by shifts in yield levels.
5. When yields are high, shifts in yield will have a much greater impact on the income of investors and lenders and on the costs to borrowers than when yields are low because the shifts tend to be proportional to the level of yields.

6.   The proportional effect of interest rate changes is un-
     affected by the level of yields.

The Frequency Distribution of Interest Rates

Chapter 7   Frequency Distributions

The frequency distributions of various measures of yields
reveal the following:

1.   The distribution of yields has too many yields in the
     center and an excess in the higher yields, suggesting
     that the log transformation may give a more sym-
     metrical distribution.
2.   The distribution of the logs of yields is more sym-
     metrical, more normal.
3.   The distribution of changes in yields is peaked with
     wide tails.
4.   The distribution of first differences in the logs of
     yields is also peaked, with wide tails, and symmetri-
     cal. The mean is very close to zero.

The cumulative frequency distributions reveal the same
pattern and suggest that:

1.   The expected change in yields is zero.
2.   Small changes in yields are much more likely than
     moderate changes.
3.   Extreme changes in yields, plus or minus, are more
     common than we would expect from a normal dis-
     tribution.

*Chapter 8   Is the Distribution of Interest Rates Normal
             or Log Normal?*

The following is clear from our examination of the distribution of yields and the distribution of changes in yields and
their log transforms.

1. The distribution of yields and the logs of yields is not normal.
2. The distribution of changes in yields and changes in the logs of yields is approximately normal.
3. The approximate normality of changes in yields and the logs of yields suggests that the series may be random.

The Mean Change in Yields

Chapter 9   Is the Mean Change Significantly Different from Zero?

We may conclude the following:

1. The mean change interest rates is not significantly different from zero.
2. The mean change in the logarithms of interest rates is not significantly different from zero.
3. If we wish to forecast the change in interest rates, our best estimate is no change. The most recent interest rate is the best estimate of the next rate.

Chapter 10   The Standard Error of the Mean

The principal characteristics of the mean change in the logs of interest rates where n is the number of units of time used to calculate the mean are the following:

1. Past and future mean changes in yield show a great deal of variability.
2. The longer the period over which the mean is calculated, the less the degree of variability in the means. The variability of the means declines with n.
3. The standard deviation of the means of changes in the logs of yields declines with the number of months used in calculating the means.
4. The average standard error of the means declines with the square root of n ($s/n^{.5}$).

The Dispersion of Interest Rates

2. The standard deviation of changes in the logarithms of interest rates rises approximately with the square root of the difference interval.

3. The rise in the standard deviation does not appear to level off.

4. The relationship appears to hold for various types of issues, yield series, individual bonds, corporates, and governments.

5. The relationship does not appear to depend on the frequency of measurement; it holds where the minimum interval is as short and as one day and as long as a year.

6. The relationship represents evidence that changes in the logarithms of interest rates are random.

Chapter 14   The Standard Deviation of Changes in the Logarithms of Interest Rates Rises with Maturity

By examining the combined effect of maturity and time on the standard deviation of yields, we are able to derive formulas that permit us to estimate future volatility. Volatility is higher over longer forecast periods and higher for shorter maturity bonds. This relationship is true of nearly all bond series and historical eras.

1. The standard deviation of changes in the logs of interest rates rises approximately with the square root of the difference interval, or holding period.

2. The standard deviation of changes in the logs of interest rates declines with the maturity of the bond.

3. For U.S. Government bonds in the period 1950 to 1986, the equation is:

$$\text{standard deviation} = .27 \, (\text{difference interval})^{.40} / (\text{maturity})^{.28}$$

4. For U.S. corporate bonds in the period 1900-1965, the equation is:

$$\text{standard deviation} = .23 \text{ (difference interval)}^{.61} / (\text{maturity})^{.40}$$

5. The volatility of different kinds of bonds of the same maturity is similar in similar periods.
6. The historical era has more influence on volatility of interest rates than does the type bond.
7. The ability to model the volatility of interest rates as a function of the difference interval (holding period) and maturity enables us to estimate the future range and distribution of interest rates and thereby estimate interest rate risk
8. With estimates of future interest rates for specific bond maturities, we can apply the formula for calculating the price of a bond, given the maturity, coupon and future yield to maturity give us the future market risk of the bond.

Chapter 15   *The Standard Deviation of Daily Changes in Interest Rates versus Maturity and the Difference Interval, 1987 Data*

1. For daily data in 1987, the standard deviation of changes in the natural logarithms of yields rises with the difference interval with a slope of 1/2. This is the same result we obtained for monthly and annual yield indexes, but now the slope coefficient much closer to 0.5.
2. The 1987 daily data does not exhibit much general relationship between the standard deviation and maturity. However, as the difference interval is increased from 1 to 20 days, a inverse relationship does begin to emerge more and more clearly as the difference interval is lengthened.

Chapter 16   How the Volatility of Changes in the Logarithms of
Rates Varies from One Historical Period to Another

1. The volatility of changes in interest rates, measured by the standard deviation of changes in the logarithms of rates, is not the same in all historical periods.

2. Most of the time, the standard deviation of changes in the logarithms of interest rates, is within a factor of 3.

3. Changes in the volatility of interest rates, changes in the standard deviation, are approximately twice as great as they are for a random series.

4. The distributions of standard deviations of changes in the natural logarithms of yields exhibit departures from normality. The way in which these standard deviations decline as the number of months used to calculate them is not typical of a purely random series.

5. Thus, the overall evidence, based on this data, is that there is some coincidence between periods of high and low volatility of short-bonds and long-bonds, but not very much.

The Comovement of Interest Rates

Chapter 17   The Comovement of Interest Rates of Different
Maturities

1. There is a great deal of comovement in changes in yields among bonds of different maturities. When yields rise, they tend to rise for all maturities, and when yields fall, they tend to fall for all maturities.

2. The comovement is statistically significant.

3. Comovement accounts for the majority of the variability of changes in interest rates. The influence of time on the volatility of interest rates is very large.

4. The influence of maturity on the total variability of changes in interest rates is relatively small.
5. There is very little autocorrelation of changes in yields. In other words, the change in rates in one period has very little to do with changes in other periods.

Chapter 18   Changes in Yield by Maturity, U.S. Government Bonds and Notes, 1987

The following is based on this daily data for 1987:

1. Over short difference intervals of a day or a few days, there is no relationship between the degree of change in yields and the maturity of the bond.
2. Over long periods, there is a striking relationship between the maturity of the bond and the degree of change in yields.
3. The time, or difference interval, required to achieve a relationship between degree of change and maturity varies sharply, from 6 days to 100 days, for the above data.
4. The relationship between degree of change in yields and maturity is approximate.
5. The existence of the relationship between the maturity of the bond and the degree of change in yields is sufficient to explain the formation of the yield curve.

Chapter 19   Cross-Sectional Dispersion of Daily U.S. Government Yields

Several observations can be made about the cross sectional standard deviation of changes in the logs in yields:

1. The cross-sectional standard deviation is positive.
2. It rises approximately with the square root of time.
3. It continues to rise for at least a year, based on daily data for 1987.

4. The rise is intermittent, not continuous.

5. The cross-sectional standard deviation for a given difference interval is only about one-fifth as large as the sequential standard deviation for the same difference interval.

6. That it is positive and continuous forms evidence for the randomness of changes in interest rates.

Chapter 20   Random Changes in the Yield Curve

1. Although long and short rates tend to move up and down together, short rates move more.

2. A consequence of the greater comovement of short rates is that when rates rise, the slope of the yield curve rises, and when rates fall, the slope of the yield curve falls.

3. The change in rates, up or down, appears to be a random variable so that changes in the slope of the yield curve must also be a random variable, whether measured by the actual slope of the yield curve or measured by the difference in the natural logarithms of the ratio of short bond yields to long-bond yields.

4. Since most of the changes in the yield curve are caused by the greater movement of short rates, changes in the yield curve are largely a function of changes in short bond rates.

5. We should be able to calculate the probability of a reversal in the slope of the yield curve from the difference between long and short rates and the standard deviation of the difference between changes in long and short rates.

6. The standard deviation of changes in the logarithms of the ratio of short-bond to long-bond rates rises with the difference interval at somewhat less than the square root value, but nonetheless in conformance with a random walk.

Chapter 21   Lead Lag Relationships

1. There is very little lead or lag cross-correlation between changes in yields of different maturities, based on monthly, weekly, and daily data.

The Dispersion of Bond Prices

Chapter 22   Individual Bonds—Prices and Yields

1. Based on the data for 1987 U.S. government bonds, the price volatility of longer bonds exceeds that of shorter bonds.
2. The yield volatility is the same for short and long issues for this set of bonds and this period, 1987.

Chapter 23   The Dispersion of Individual Bond Prices and Yields

1. The standard deviation of changes in prices is a rising function of maturity—the longer the maturity, the higher the value of s.
2. The standard deviation of changes in the logs of yields is a very slightly falling function of maturity—the lower the maturity, the higher s.
3. The standard deviation of changes in yields is always higher than the standard deviation of changes in prices, by definition and by observation.
4. The volatility of yield of every maturity is higher than the volatility of price of any maturity.
5. There are a number of outliers, or exceptions to the general trend. Some of these outliers are bonds with very low coupons.

Other Evidence of Randomness

Chapter 24   Tests of Randomness—Signs Tests

The following conclusions apply on the assumption that the expected number of changes in the series is zero.

1. In the British consol series, 1730 to 1961, the number of increases does not differ significantly from one half the total number of changes, suggesting randomness.

2. In the Durand data, 1900 to 1965, the number of increases is close to one half, again suggesting randomness.

3. In the Salomon data 1950 to 1986, there are more increases than expected.

4. In the Macaulay data 1857 to 1936, there are fewer increases than expected.

5. Significant departures constitute variances of 10% to 15% from the expected values.

6. These results suggest that the signs of changes in yields are more often than not random. However, at times there are somewhat more increases or decreases than we would expect from a perfectly random series.

Chapter 25   Runs—More Evidence of Randomness

1. For the most part, first differences in the logs of yields are random.

2. The yields themselves are not random.

3. Changes in yields are not random.

4. This evidence supplements the evidence from the signs tests, confirming that changes in the logs of interest rates are random.

Chapter 26   Signed Rankings

1. The signed rank tests show that the distributions were symmetric with respect to the median for all series and with respect to zero for most, providing further evidence of randomness.

Chapter 27   Autocorrelation of Interest Rates and Changes in Interest Rates

1. For yields, the coefficients of autocorrelation decline slowly, reaching zero for the monthly series after a decade or two.
2. For first differences in yields, the coefficients of autocorrelation are generally not significant after lag 0, indicating randomness.
3. For first differences in the logarithms of yields, the coefficients of autocorrelation is not significant after lag 0.
4. The lack of autocorrelation for changes in yields is indicative of randomness.

Chapter 28   Spectral Analysis

1. Based on periodogram analysis, there appear to be no significant periodicity in the yield series or in first differences in the logs of yields, the only exception being some departures for the 1857 to 1936 data.
2. The plot of seasonality reveals no significant seasonality.

Chapter 29   Short-Term Forecasting of Interest Rates

1. Modern forecasting models are able to fit the past values of unpredictable series (random walks) almost perfectly.
2. How well a model fits past data is not a sufficient criteria of future forecasting accuracy for interest rate series. For economic series in general, how well the model fits past data is not related to how well the model forecasts the future. Other criteria are necessary.
3. There must be some form of regularity in a series, periodic or cyclic, seasonal, or trend, to allow ac-

curate forecasts. Without such regularity, it is not possible to forecast changes in the series with any accuracy.

4.   The models that have provided the best fits to past interest data are autoregressive schemes which are, or are very close to, random walk models [ARIMA(1,1,0)]. This closeness is not only evidence for the random walk model, but evidence for the inability to forecast future rates.

Chapter 30   Interest Rates and Inflation

1.   The ratio of interest rates to wholesale prices is a random walk based on 1750 to 1961 British annual data.

2.   The ratio of short-term interest rates to the consumer price index is a random walk, based on U.S. 1950 to 1986 monthly data.

3.   The U.S. consumer price index is not a random walk over the 1950 to 1986 period.

4.   Since the ratio of interest rates to wholesale and consumer prices appears to be a random walk, there doesn't appear to be much relationship between interest rates and inflation.

Appendix I

A Contrast of Linear, Periodic, and Random Series

Most of the evidence of this book is presented in graphs of the data, graphs designed to show whether or not the data is random. In order to see whether the data is random, it is essential to know what a random series looks like in different kinds of graphs and how those graphs contrast with graphs of linear data and periodic data.

The two most prominent nonrandom series are the linear series and the periodic series. Any linear series may by appropriate transformations be reduced to the set of integers 1, 2, . . ., n. Any periodic series may by other transformations be reduced to a set of sine curves. So that the different graphs of these three series—linear, periodic, and random—may be clear, we present graphs of each series.

Linear Series

A linear series is the most common type of series. It follows the form 1, 2, 3, . . ., n, most commonly associated with the set of integers. When graphed, a linear series forms a straight line, hence, the designation linear. Any linear series can be converted into the set of integers (1, 2, 3, . . .) by adding the appropriate constant to and multiplying by the appropriate factor each item in the series. In other words, any linear series may be modeled by the formula $y = a + bx$.

We can best understand the characteristics of ideal series like yield series if we have a good understanding of the graphs of a linear series. Figure A.1 shows the original linear series, first difference in the series, the logs of the series, first differences in the logs, the estimated autocorrelation of the series, and a periodogram. The series itself forms a straight line; first differences form a constant; the logs represent a curve that rises sharply and bends to the right, monotonically increasing; and the first difference in the logs form a monotonically decreasing series. For the figure, we used the series 1, 2, 3, . . ., 300.

Graph E in Figure A.1 gives the estimated autocorrelation of a linear series, or the correlogram. The autocorrelations were not computed using the formula found in most statistical packages, including the one used for these figures, and described in Kendall, and other books on time-series analysis. That formula uses the variance for the total series to find the coefficients, partly because the computation is less complicated and partly because the variance of the whole may be a better estimate of variance.

These reasons are less important, however, than the fact that the short formula gives coefficients for a linear series that are incorrect. The coefficients, which should be 1 for all lags, will decline with the lag to zero and below. For a perfectly linear series, the correct coefficient of correlation at all lags, as shown in Figure A.1, is 1.0. All of the variation is explained by the linear formula $y = a + bx$ and all coefficients of determination are 1.

The coefficients Figure A.1 were calculated using the standard regression formula with the appropriate segments of the series as the dependent and independent variables. The periodogram of the series is shown in Graph F of Figure A.1. Graphs A through D should be kept in mind for comparison with the various graphs of the interest rate series. The differences are substantial.

Figure A.1   Time Series Plots of Linear Series

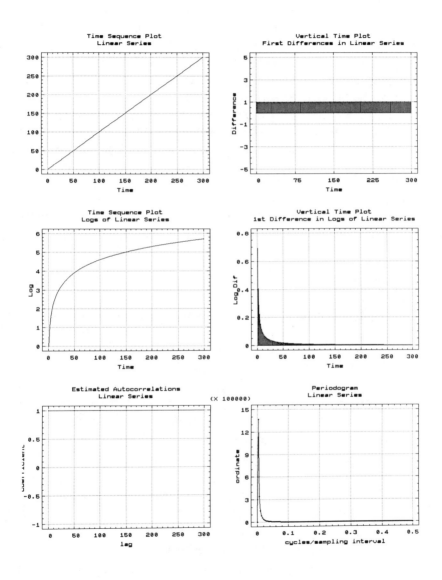

Figure A.2 gives the frequency distributions of the original linear series, first differences, logs, and first differences in logs. These graphs are again very different from the corresponding graphs of the interest rate series. Graph E gives the cumulative distribution. The distribution of the series is rectangular, and the distribution of the first difference is the frequency of a single number, all ones in this case. If the series were log linear, then the graphs of the logs would behave as the graphs of a linear series.

Figure A.3 gives the seasonal subseries plot, the integrated periodogram, the plot versus Fourier frequencies, and the standard deviation of changes in the logs of the series versus the difference interval. Clearly, there is no seasonality in the series. The periodogram value of 1 is outside the confidence intervals, indicating a nonrandom series. The standard deviation is zero for all difference intervals. This is substantially different than what we find with interest rates.

Summary

A linear series has a number of distinctive characteristics:

1.   The graph of the series itself and of first differences in the series form a straight line.
2.   The graph of the logs forms a series that rises at a decreasing rate, and the graph of first differences in the logs forms a graph that falls at a decreasing rate.
3.   The correlogram forms a straight line at 1.
4.   The periodogram has a single peak.
5.   The frequency distribution of the series is flat at the top, and the frequency distribution of changes is single valued.
6.   The frequency distribution of the logs rises and that of changes in the logs falls, both at decreasing rates.
7.   The seasonal graph shows no periodicity but simply a rising or falling trend.

Figure A.2 Histograms of Linear Series

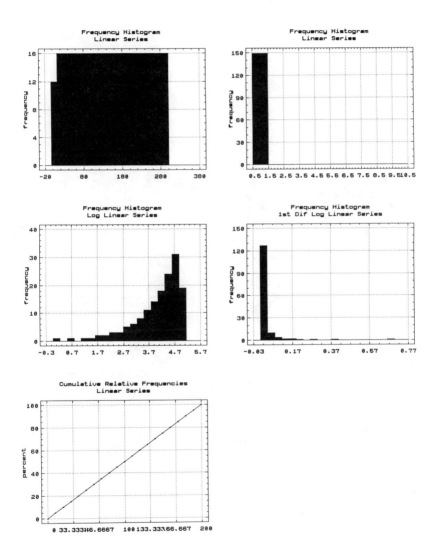

Figure A.3   Time Series Plots of Linear Series

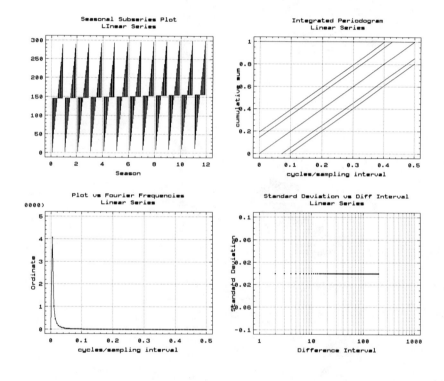

8. The standard deviation of changes in the logs of the series is a horizontal line of zero.

Periodic Series

A regular periodic series is a series that oscillates in a regular way with a fixed period and a fixed amplitude. A good example is a simple harmonic motion, which may be represented by the sine curve shown in Graph A, Figure A.4. This curve varies between +1 and -1. It can be modeled by the equation $y = \sin x$, where x is measured in radians and varies between 0 and 2 pi. This curve has a constant amplitude and period.

Graph B of Figure A.4 gives the plot of first differences in the sine curve. The amplitude of differences is less, but the period is the same as that of the original curve, approximately a sine curve.

Graph C illustrates the estimated autocorrelation, or correlogram, of the sine curve. The coefficient varies from +1 to -1 with the same period as the original sine curve but with a different phase angle. The difference in phase angle is pi/2. The periodogram has a single peak. Graph F shows the seasonal subseries plot and indicates the perfect periodicity of the series. To obtain this plot, it is necessary to know the period.

Figure A.5 gives the integrated periodogram (A) and the standard deviation of changes in the logs of the series plotted against the difference interval (B). The points on the integrated periodogram are all outside the confidence interval, indicating a nonrandom series. The standard deviation of changes in the logs ranges between approximately 1 and 0. It has a period that is equal to that of the original series. The log log plot, which is used comparison with the yield series, gives the erroneous appearance of an irregular period. On an arithmetic scale, the series would appear regular.

For simple periodicity, the graphs reveal periodicity in the original series, in first differences in the series, in autocorrelations, in the seasonal subseries plot, and in the standard

Figure A.4 Time Series Plots of Simple Sine Series

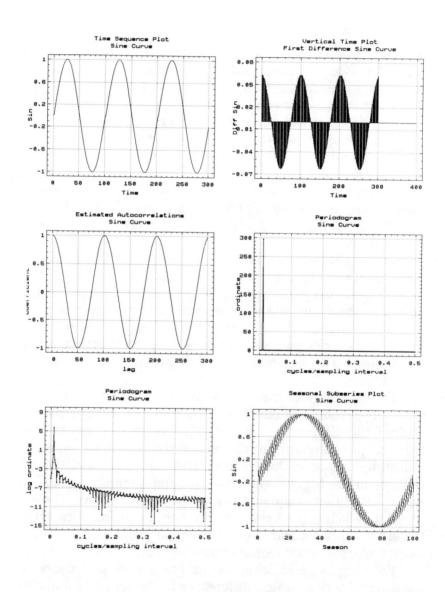

Figure A.5 Time Series Plots of Simple Sine Series

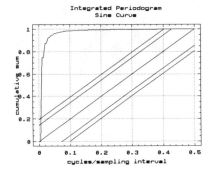

Integrated Periodogram
Sine Curve

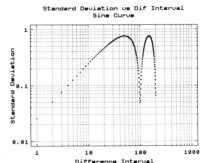

Standard Deviation vs Dif Interval
Sine Curve

deviation of changes versus the difference interval. Each of these feature is clearly revealed in the graphs.

Periodic series of different amplitudes and different periods can be added together to form more complex yet equally periodic series. Figure A.6 gives the sum of three sine curves. Graph A shows the resultant figure, and Graph C shows the three sine series that formed it together with the resultant series. As you can see, each of the three component series is a pure sine series but of a different period and amplitude. The plot of first differences reveals the periodicity of the series, as does the seasonal subseries plot. The estimated autcorrelations shows the periodicity of the series.

Figure A.6 Time Series Plots of Sum of Sine Series

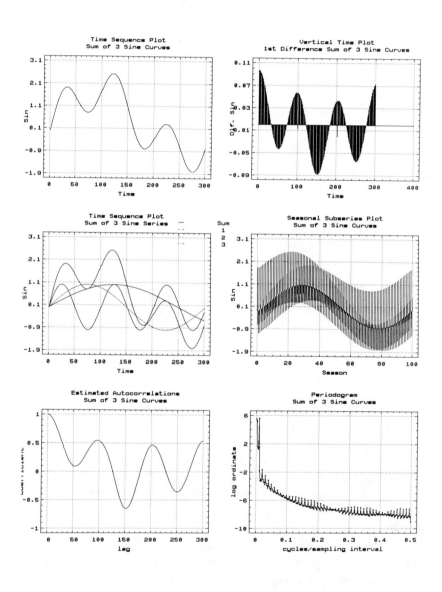

Graph A of Figure A.7 shows separate peaks, and Graph B, the indicated periodogram shows that the series is clearly not random, since nearly all of the points are outside the bounds. Graph D reveals periodicity in the series, as shown by what appears to be an upper boundary in the dispersion of the series.

Summary

A periodic series has the following distinctive characteristics.

1. The graphs of the series and of first differences in the series are periodic with fixed amplitudes and periods.
2. The autocorrelation function is periodic, ranging in value from +1 to -1.
3. The periodogram has a single peak.
4. The seasonal plot is periodic.
5. The integrated periodogram lies outside the normal confidence interval, indicating nonrandomness.
6. The standard deviation of differences in the series is periodic and except for the first phase does not increase with the square root of time.
7. Combinations of sine curves having different amplitudes and periods exhibit many of the above characteristics, though the periodogram has more than one peak and the cycles are less regular.

Random Series

Purely random series are characterized by an absence trend, linear or otherwise, and no periodicity. The magnitude and direction of future elements cannot be predicted from past elements, except in the probability sense.

Figure A.7   Time Series Plots of Sum of Sine Series

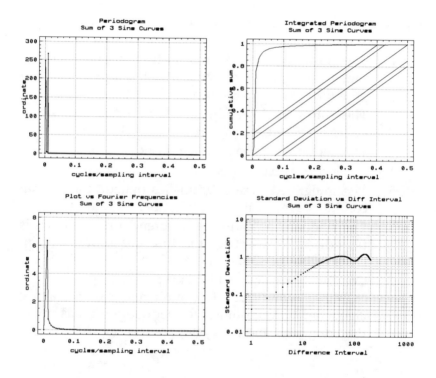

An ideal random series may be generated by flipping a coin and assigning +1 to heads and -1 to tails. If we form a running cumulation of the series, we obtain a random walk. Such a series is sometimes referred to as a Markov series. We can describe the variables as follows:

$$y = \log_e x \tag{1}$$
$$\Delta x = x\,(t + 1) - x\,(t) \tag{2}$$
$$\Delta y = y\,(t + 1) - y\,(t) = \log_e x\,(t + 1) - \log_e x\,(t) \tag{3}$$

When we simulate a series using random numbers, Δx is the original variable and $x\,(t = n)$ is the sum of $\Delta x\,(t)$ from $t = 0$ to $t = n$. The variable $y\,(t)$ is exp $x\,(t)$. When we take the logs of y we obtain x and when we take first differences in x we obtain the original random variable.

The random series (x) has a number of characteristics:

1. The direction of the next change, positive or negative, cannot be predicted any more than the flip of a coin.
2. The series itself (x) may exhibit what appear to be trends and cycles (i.e., linear and periodic components), but these are illusions and give no indication as to future direction or movement.
3. The distribution of the cumulative series (x) will generally be normal but does not need to be; normal and generally will not be.
4. The distribution of changes in the series (Δx) will tend to be normal.
5. The standard deviation of changes in the series (Δx) will rise with the square root of the number of elements.
6. The first difference series (Δx) will be stationary or invariant over time with respect to the mean and the variance.

If we take the antilogs of the running sum of the results of coin tossing, we obtain a new series (y) that differs from the underlying cumulative series in the following respects:

1. Changes in scale occur so that the series appears to have more pronounced trends than would be the case if antilogs were not taken.
2. The taking of antilogs by changing the scale of the series is likely to produce shifts in volatility so the series is heteroscedastic, the variance is not stationary.

The antilog series (y), as well as the series (x) from which it was formed, have features that seem contrary to common sense. If the first cumulative element is positive, the most likely event is that all future elements will be positive. The most likely number of returns to the origin is zero, the next most likely is one, and so on. The probability of getting two identical sequences in 10,000 tosses of a coin is only 1 in 10,000. While the probability of ending up at the origin in the cumulation of 10,000 is the most likely outcome, that probability is small. Series R2 was formed by simulating the flipping of coins using the Basic random-number generator. The coins were flipped, the plus and minus ones were accumulated in a running sum, and the antilogs of the running sum were taken to create random series R2. The series R2 is equivalent to series y above.

Figure A.8 shows the original series R2 and its components. Graphs A, B, C, and D show the original series, first differences in the original series, the logs of the original series, and first differences in the logs of the series. Series r2a is simply the first 250 elements of series r2 that contained 1000 elements.

Graph A, Figure A.8, shows the antilogs of the cumulative series; this pattern resembles those of interest rates and bond prices. Graph B shows first differences in the Graph A data. Note that the volatility is lower in the first part of the series and higher in the last part. Clearly, the volatility is not invariant over time.

Graph C gives the logarithms of the first series, and Graph D gives first differences in the logs. This first difference panel has equal volatility throughout, as we would expect.

Figure A.8   Time Series Plots of Random Series

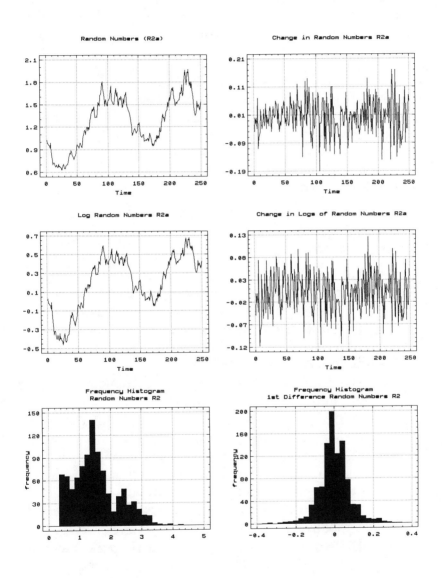

The frequency distributions, shown at the bottom, are clearly not symmetrical for the original series, and therefore not normal but symmetrical for the first differences.

Figure A.9 gives other measures of the distributions. The seasonal subseries plot (A) reveals no seasonality, or periodicity; the periodogram (B) shows a single peak; and the integrated periodogram (D) reveals a random series, since the entire line is within the confidence interval. Graph F shows how the standard deviation of first differences in the logs of r2 rises with the square root of time. There is no leveling off, or periodicity, apparent in the series.

Summary

The following characteristics describe a random walk formed by cumulating random variables and taking the exponents of the resulting series.

1. The graph of the series (y) is irregular, yet may appear to exhibit trends and cycles and shifts in scale.
2. The graph of first differences (Δy) in the series will appear random with approximately as many increases as decreases. This graph may also show changes in volatility.
3. The graph of the logs (x) of the variable may appear to exhibit trends and cycles, but not shifts in scale.
4. The graph of first differences in the logs (Δx) of the variable will appear random with constant variance.
5. The histogram of the series (y) may not appear normal but the histogram of first differences in the logs of the series (Δx) will appear normal.
6. None of the series will exhibit seasonal or periodic components.
7. The periodogram will have a single peak integrated periodogram will not fall outside the normal bounds.
8. The standard deviation of changes in the logs of the series (Δx) will rise with the square root of time.

Figure A.9   Time Series Plots of Random Series

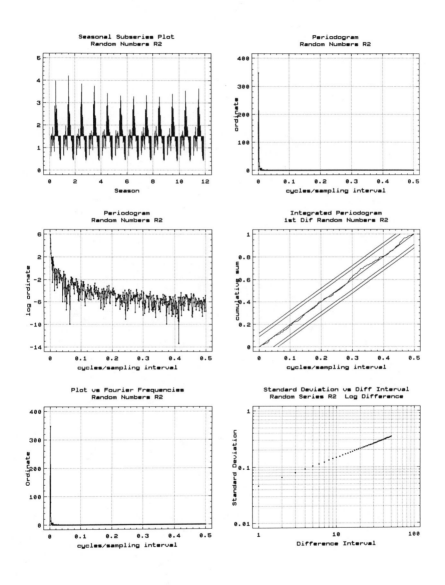

References

Aitchison, J. and Brown, J. A. C., *The Lognormal Distribution with Special Reference to its Uses in Economics*, Cambridge University Press, London, 1981.

Barry, J. V. and Ayres, H. E., "A Theory of the U.S. Treasury Market Equilibrium," *Management Science*, Vol. 26, No. 6, (June 1980), pp. 539-569.

Bachelier, *Theory of Speculation*, Gauthier-Villers, Paris 1900 (translated in Cootner).

Brick, John R. and Thompson, Howard E., "Time Series Analysis of Interest Rates: Some Additional Evidence," *Journal of Finance*, Vol. 33, No. 1 (March 1978), pp. 93-103.

Brown, Stephen J. and Dybvig, Philip H., "The Empirical Implications of the Cox, Ingersoll, Ross Theory of the Term Structure of Interest Rates," *Journal of Finance*, Vol. 41, No. 3 (July 1986), pp. 617-632.

Cargill, Thomas F. and Meyer, Robert A., "A Spectral Approach to Estimating the Distributed Lag Relationship Between Long and Short Term Interest Rates," *International Economic Review*, (June 1972), pp. 223-238.

Cootner, P. E., *The Random Character of Stock Market Prices*, MIT Press, Cambridge, Mass., 1964

Fand, David I., "A Time-Series Analysis of the 'Bills-Only' Theory of Interest Rates," *The Review of Economics and Statistics*, Vol. 48 (November 1966), pp. 361–371

Granger, C. W. J., and Rees, H. J. B, "Spectral Analysis of the Term Structure of Interest Rates," *Review of Economic Studies* (January 1968), pp. 67-75.

Hamburger, Michael J. and Latta, Cynthia M., "The Term Structure of Interest Rates" Some Additional Evidence," *Journal of Money, Credit, and Banking*, Vol. 1 (February 1969), pp. 71-83.

Hause, John C., "Spectral Analysis and the Detection of Lead-Lag Relations," *American Economic Review*, Vol. VXXI (March 1971), pp. 213-217.

Hopewell, Michael H. and Kaufman, George G., "Bond Price Volatility and Term to Maturity: A Generalized Respecification," *The American Economic Review*, Vol. 63, No. 4 (September 1972), pp. 749-753.

Kendall, M.G., *Time-Series*, 2nd edition, Hafner Press, N.Y., 1976.

Kendall, M. G. and Stewart, A., *The Advanced Theory of Statistics*, Vol. 1, 4th edition, MacMillan, New York, 1977.

Kendall, M. G. and Stewart, A., *The Advanced Theory of Statistics*, Vol. 2, 2nd edition, Hafner, New York, 1973.

Mandelbrot, B., "The Variation of Certain Speculative Prices," *Journal of Business*, Vol. 36, 1963, pp. 395-419. Also in Cootner.

Marsh, Terry A. and Rosenfeld, Eric R., "Stochastic Processes for Interest Rates and Equilibrium Bond Prices," *Journal of Finance*, Vol. 38, No. 2 (May 1983), pp. 635-650.

Modigliani, Franco and Sutch, Richard, "The Term Structure of Interest Rates: A Reexamination of the Evidence," *Journal of Money, Credit, and Banking*, Vol. 1 (February 1969), pp. 112-120.

Modigliani, Franco, and Shiller, Robert, "Inflation, Rational Expectations and the Term Structure of Interest Rates," *Economica*, Vol. 40 (February 1973), pp. 12–43.

Murphy, J. E., *With Interest: How to Profit from Fluctuations in Interest Rates*, Dow-Jones Irwin, Chicago, Ill., 1986.

Murphy, J. E. and Osborne, M. F. M., "Brownian Motion in the Bond Market," *The Review of Futures Markets*, Vol. 6, No. 3 (December 1987), 306-326.

Murphy, J. E. and Osborne, M. F. M., "Predicting the Volatility of Interest Rates," *Journal of Portfolio Management*, Winter 1985, pp. 66-69.

Osborne, M. F. M., "Random Walks in Earnings and Fixed Income Securities," Seminar, Institute for Quantitative Research in Finance, April, 1968. Available from the Institute, Columbia University, New York, N.Y.

Osborne, M. F. M., *The Stock Market and Finance from a Physicist's Viewpoint*, published by the author (1977), 3803 24th Avenue, Temple Hills, MD, 20748.

Phillips, Llad and Pippenger, John, "Preferred Habitat vs. Efficient Market: A Test of Alternative Hypotheses," *Federal Reserve Bank of St. Louis Review*, Vol. 58 (May 1976), pp. 11-19.

Pippenger, John, "A Time Series Analysis of Post Accord Interest Rates: A Comment," *Journal of Finance*, Vol. 29 (September 1974), pp. 1320-1325.

Roll, Richard, *The Behavior of Interest Rates*, New York, Basic Books, 1970.

Smith, V. Kerry and Marcis, Richard G., "A Time Series Analysis of Post-Accord Interest Rates," *Journal of Finance*, Vol. 27 (June 1972), pp. 589-605.

Smith, V. Kerry and Marcis, Richard G., "Post Accord Interest Rates: A Reply," *Journal of Finance*, Vol. 29 (September 1974), pp. 1326-1327.

Wood, John A., "The Expectations Hypothesis, the Yield Curve, and Monetary Policy," *Quarterly Journal of Economics*, Vol. 78 (August 1964), pp. 457-470.

Data Sources

Durand, David, *Basic Yields of Corporate Bonds, 1900-1942*, Technical Paper 3, National Bureau of Economic Research, New York, N.Y., 1947.

Tradeline Historical Securities Information, Gregg Corporation, Waltham, Mass.

Homer, Sidney, *A History of Interest Rates*, Rutgers University Press, New Brunswick, N.J., 1963.

Macaulay, Frederick R., *The Movements of Interest Rates, Bond Yields and Stock Prices in the United States since 1856*, National Bureau of Economic Research, New York, N.Y., 1938.

Malkiel, Burton G., *The Term Structure of Interest Rates*, Princeton University Press, Princeton, N.J., 1966.

Mitchell, B. R. and Johnes, H., *Annual European Historical Statistics*.

Salomon Brothers, *An Analytical Record of Yields and Yield Spreads*, New York, N.Y., 1979, 1986.

Standard & Poor, *Security Price Index Record*, New York, N.Y.

Computer Graphics

Statgraphics, Princeton, N.J.

Index

A

Absolute change, 21
ANOVA, 170, 176
Autocorrelation of interest rates, 175, 247-53

B

Bachelier, 262
Bonds
    constant maturity bond indexes, 13
    daily changes in prices, 216
    daily prices, 214, 220
    daily yields, 215, 221
    dispersion of bond prices and yields, 219
    individual prices and yields, 209-17
    price volatility, 125-39
    yields of long bonds, 28
    British consol index, 7, 28, 35, 231
British consol yields, 76, 81, 82, 85, 90

of interest rates, 32, 151
pattern of, 28

W

Wilcox signed ranks test, 241

Y

Yields
    average annual changes in, 87
    annual corporate yields, 17
    beginning yield, 107-11
    British bonds, 19
    British consol yields, 28
    change in yields of 3-month U.S. securities, 22
    changes in yield by maturity, 183-88
    commercial paper/long-bond, 200
    correlation of 3-month and 20-year yields, 158
    correlation of commercial paper and long-term, 159
    curve, 12, 187, 189, 193-202
    difference interval, 143-44
    differences in Logarithms of, 117
    historical yields, 25, 27
    frequency of increases, 107-08
    level of, 50, 52
    number of increases in, 230-231
    random changes in yield curve, 193-202
    ratio of ending to beinning yields vs. maturity, 185-86
    since Civil War, 45
    short-bond/long-bond, 195, 197-98
    three-month/20-year yields, 199
    U.S. bond yields, 12, 28, 67, 189
    U.S. securities, 13
    U.S. government yields, 14, 33, 197
Yule, 262